W9-COX-868

CONTENTS

INTRODUCTION

BOTANICALLY SPEAKING

Beans, peas, and lentils, collectively known as legumes, are the edible seeds contained in a single row inside the pods of a huge group of flowering vines or bushes called leguminous plants.

Grains are the edible seeds, or kernels, of a wide variety of grasses known as cereal grasses.

Still lingering in the far reaches of my memory is the unique taste of the butter beans cooked by Mamaw Olivia Bell Keith, my maternal grandmother, on a wood-burning stove in her wonderful old Mississippi plantation house. Maybe it was the fragrant wood fuel, or the homegrown freshly shelled beans, or the succulent seasoning of pork from her smokehouse that etched those beans so indelibly in my mind. More likely, as with most romanticized recollections of foods enjoyed in the distant past, it was the comfort that came with dining around Mamaw's kitchen table.

Considering the quantity that I've consumed over the years, I should know my beans by now. While growing up, our family meals featured some sort of legume several times a week. During the summer we enjoyed creamy brown crowder peas that were shared by Daddy's parishioners in bushel baskets stocked from their nearby fields, and fresh butter beans that Mother still cooks as well as Mamaw Keith did. Green beans were simmered for hours with bacon or salt pork in black iron pots until they were drab olive, soft, and sublime tasting (in the intervening years, my skeptical friends who thought green beans should only be bright green and crisp have all succumbed to those southern-style beans, which have been dubbed Green Beans Lucy in honor of my mother). To accompany Daddy's barbecues, Mother always made a big dish of sweet-and-tangy baked beans. During cold weather, we'd enjoy more of those summer peas and butter beans from the freezer, or our maid, Savannah, would transform big, fat dried limas into one of the most savory feasts I've ever enjoyed.

Living in New Orleans during and after graduate school days, I immediately adapted to the Monday custom of eating red beans. And wherever I have lived since, from New York to California, I have cooked and eaten my beans regularly. My world of bean cookery has grown dramatically over the years, as the vast array of types, colors, and sizes consumed beyond my home has become more readily available. I can now choose from creamy white *cannellini* from Italy, pale green-tinged *flageolets* from France, olive-green mung beans from China, dark red *azuki* from Japan, salmon-hued *masoor* lentils from India, tawny beige garbanzos from the Middle East, and a host of beans from the American continents: maroon cranberry, cream to green lima, dark red kidney, deep purple scarlet runner, and jet-black turtle beans. Varieties and hybrids appear with a wide range of spots or eyes, splashes, and patterns. And some of the picturesque names add humor in my kitchen as I decide whether to cook a pot of Tongues of Fire, Soldiers, Jacob's Cattle, Whippoorwills, Appaloosas, Calypsos, Calicos, Pebbles, Rattlesnakes, or Wren's Eggs.

Of course, whenever I've enjoyed all these beans over the years, they have never been consumed on their own. Back home, we always spooned the flavorful cooking liquid from the beans, known to southerners as "pot licker," over our ubiquitous golden cornbread. And there was plenty of fluffy white rice, fresh corn, hominy, or grits alongside the beans. Even now I rarely serve beans without a big pot of quinoa or another grain, or a warm batch of cornbread or tortillas to accompany them.

Since the discovery of fire, good cooks have known instinctively that beans need their grain partners, both for enjoyment and good nutrition. Grains traditionally have been called "the fuel of civilization" and have held the top position as the most important food in our diet from the beginning of history. While all civilizations have cultivated one or a handful of beans, some type of grain or grain product has reigned as their staff of life—rice in Asia, sorghum and millet in central Africa, teff in eastern Africa, couscous in northern Africa, buckwheat in eastern Europe, oats in the British Isles, and corn in the Americas.

Early settlers to the New World brought with them the grains of their homelands, most of which flourished here. Yet North Americans have come to favor white flour refined from wheat and highly processed forms of other grains over the often tastier and more nutritious whole grains of our forefathers. But through the efforts of modern nutritionists and our expanding global awareness of food, the wide world of grains is being discovered and rediscovered. My own grain pantry now includes an array of these ancient staples, which I always look forward to cooking and introducing to friends and family.

These days in the Napa Valley, far from Catahoula Parish in Louisiana, I relish the flavorful white beans at Jan Birnbaum's nationally acclaimed Catahoula (a restaurant named for the dog native to my childhood home), the lentil cassoulet at Fred Halpert's award-winning Brava Terrace, and the bed of spicy black beans served under a perfectly grilled chicken breast at Cindy Pawlcyn's famous Mustards Grill. Humble grains have also been elevated to a new status as part of today's upscale cuisine; rice now stars as *risotto* and cornmeal mush earns new respect when dubbed *polenta.* It has been exciting to watch my beloved beans and grains move from simple country fare to the hallowed halls of gourmet dining establishments. Innovative chefs and good home cooks everywhere now hold beans and grains with great regard and feature them in flavorful dishes and stylish presentations.

Nutritional Powerhouses

Simply put, protein is the building material found in every cell of the body and it must be replenished daily for good health. Beans and other legumes contain the highest percentage of protein of any vegetable, and grains also contain a goodly share. And with most dried beans selling for under a dollar per pound and many grains costing merely pennies per pound, their proteins are the most inexpensive forms available.

The amino acids found in protein are used in numerous ways to form different types of cell structures: bone, cartilage, muscle, blood, lymph, skin, hair, and nails. Nine of the twenty-two amino acids are classed as *essential* because they cannot be manufactured by the body and thus must be obtained from the foods we eat. Legumes, except soybeans, contain eight of these essential amino acids, lacking only methionine; soybeans boast all nine. Fortunately, methionine is plentiful in grains, so when teamed together, beans and grains compete with meats in both quantity and quality of protein.

Both legumes and grains are naturally low in fat, cholesterol free, and packed with vitamins, minerals, and beneficial enzymes. They are also rich in complex carbohydrates, which fuel the body when stored as glycogen in the muscle tissue and liver, waiting to be broken down into glucose or blood sugar as needed. Fortunately, for those of us who love eating, the body can only store enough glycogen for a few hours at a time, so we need to replenish our fuel by consuming carbohydrates several times a day.

Dried legumes and whole grains are also loaded with fiber, both soluble and insoluble. Soluble fiber lowers cholesterol and helps to keep blood sugar levels stable. Current medical research indicates that a single cup of cooked beans a day can reduce blood cholesterol levels by an average of 10 percent (soybeans or their products can lower cholesterol levels even further), and additional studies suggest that the daily consumption of beans keeps blood glucose levels down more effectively than bran cereals, which is good news for diabetics. Insoluble fiber passes through the large intestine virtually intact and helps move all food through the digestive tract faster, disposing of some of the fat and protein consumed before they are absorbed into the body. Researchers suggest that this may help prevent colon cancer. A fiber-rich, starchy carbohydrate diet with generous amounts of beans and grains also helps control weight because the necessary long chewing satisfies the appetite with less food and the fibrous bulk actually fills you up sooner.

Beans and other legumes combined with whole grains offer not only a healthful way of eating, but also a wealth of exciting flavors and an infinite variety of preparations to the meal planner. A big pot of cooked dried beans and/or a pan of cooked grains can be served together for a delicious meal on their own, or divided for use over several days in a variety of tasty starters, comforting soups, hearty salads, satisfying main dishes, or scrumptious desserts.

USING THIS BOOK

I've divided the recipes into two sections. In BASICS you will find directions for cooking any fresh or dried bean and any available grain separately. I urge a comprehensive reading of the recipes for Cooked Dried Beans and Cooked Grains in this section, for they thoroughly explain the techniques for cooking these packets of nutrition.

Learning to cook any bean or any grain opens up a vast world of possibilities for creating your own combinations or for using the COMBINATIONS section of this book. There you will find recipes that pair beans and grains for every course from enticing appetizers through innovative desserts. Some of my favorite bean-and-grain combinations have already appeared in other volumes of this series; for your convenience, an index to those recipes is included at the end of this book.

BASICS

Fresh Beans and Peas

Indulge in fresh beans and peas at the height of their growing seasons.

When harvesting or buying, look for unshriveled crisp pods with bright, even color and no blemishes or spots. Refrigerate in loose plastic bags on the lower shelves or in the vegetable crisper and cook within a few days.

Asian long beans *(Vigna unguiculata* subspecies *sesquipedalis).* Also called Chinese long, yard-long, or asparagus beans, these Southeast Asian native green beans grow up to 2 feet in length and are a major ingredient in Chinese and other Asian cuisines. They can be used interchangeably with green beans.

Edible pod peas *(Pisum sativum* varieties). Two varieties of green peas (see later entry)—vintage snow peas and recently hybridized Sugar Snap peas— produce tender, edible pods; Sugar Snaps may be shelled as green (English) peas are or consumed pods and all as snow peas are.

Green beans *(Phaseolus vulgaris).* Also commonly known as string or snap beans, these young edible pods are members of the kidney bean family. Thankfully, modern hybridization has bred out most of the strings that had to be pulled off before cooking in the past. Interesting variations include yellow wax beans, purple pod beans, broad Italian or Romano beans, scarlet runner beans, and slender French *haricots verts.*

Green (English) peas *(Pisum sativum).* Peas originated in China, then traveled to Europe along with silk and spices. Also called garden peas, or *petits pois* in France, shelled green peas are at their sweetest and best early in the season when they are young and tender.

Shell beans. Many of the beans listed under Dried Legumes (pages 14-15) are available fresh locally during a brief season in summer. Check local farmers' markets or stands for such delicacies as fresh butter beans, black-eyed peas, cranberry beans, fava beans, soybeans, and others in your area.

Winged beans *(Psophocarpus tetrangonolobus).* A recent newcomer to our shores from Southeast Asia is the four-sided pod bean with fins running lengthwise along the connecting ridges. Known in Thailand as *tua poo,* the pale green, delicately flavored beans, which are now being grown in American tropical areas, are highly perishable.

Cooked Fresh Beans and Peas

If you have access to fresh shell beans, enjoy them when available or freeze a quantity of them. To freeze, blanch the shelled beans for 2 to 3 minutes in boiling water, then drain, pack in freezer bags, and freeze for up to 9 months.

Unlike other shell beans, fresh soybeans that are mature yet still green can be cooked in their fuzzy pods. The cooked whole pods are sometimes referred to as "popper beans" because the beans are popped out of their shells at the table. If you can't find fresh pods, look for frozen ones in Asian markets.

Today, some types of edible pod peas and green beans are available year-round, although they will have optimum flavor when picked locally in season. Local farmers' markets are an excellent source of fresh legumes.

Fresh beans or peas may be cooked by the following methods. Cooking time will vary with age and size of the legumes.

To cook shell beans (except fava beans), bring a pot of water to a boil over high heat, add the shelled beans and about 1 ounce bacon, sausage, ham, or salt pork (if using) per cup of beans, cover partially, and reduce the heat to maintain a simmer. Cook, stirring occasionally, until the beans are tender, 25 to 45 minutes, depending upon type and size. Season to taste with salt and pepper.

To cook shelled fava beans, bring a pot of water to a boil over high heat, add the shelled beans, and boil for about 3 minutes. Drain the beans, then peel off and discard the thin layer of skin from each bean. If tender, transfer to a saucepan, season to taste with salt and pepper, and reheat over medium heat. Tough peeled favas should be simmered until tender as directed for shelled beans above, then seasoned to taste.

To cook unshelled soybeans, bring a pot of water to a boil over high heat, add the whole pods, and cook until tender, 10 to 15 minutes. Drain and serve in the pods for diners to shell at the table.

→

Fresh shell beans, unshelled green soybeans, shelled green (English) peas, green beans, or edible pod peas

Sliced bacon, pork sausage, ham, or blanched salt pork (optional)

Unsalted butter for seasoning (if desired) or sautéing

Salt

Freshly ground black pepper

Olive oil or high-quality vegetable oil for sautéing or stir-frying

To blanch green beans, edible pod peas, or shelled green (English) peas for use in recipes, trim the ends and remove any strings from the beans or pea pods. Bring a pot of water to a boil over high heat and ready a bowl of iced water. When the water boils, stir in about 1 tablespoon salt, drop in the beans or peas, and cook until crisp-tender, 2 to 3 minutes. Quickly drain and transfer to the iced water to halt cooking. Drain well and use as directed.

To cook green beans, edible pod peas, or shelled green peas, trim the ends and remove any strings from the beans or pea pods. Bring a pot of water to a boil over high heat. When the water boils, stir in about 1 tablespoon salt, add the beans or peas, and cook until tender, 5 to 10 minutes. Drain, stir in a little butter to taste (if desired) and season to taste with salt and pepper. Mature green beans can also be cooked with bacon, sausage, ham, or salt pork as directed for shell beans.

To steam green beans or edible pod peas, trim the ends and remove any strings. Position a rack in a pan that will be large enough to hold the beans or peas and can be completely covered by a lid. Pour in water to a level just below the steaming rack, place over high heat, and bring to a boil, then lower the heat to maintain a simmer. Place the beans or peas on the steamer rack, cover, and steam until crisp-tender, 5 to 15 minutes. Transfer to a bowl, stir in a little butter to taste (if desired) and season to taste with salt and pepper.

To sauté green beans or edible pod peas, trim the ends and remove any strings. Cut green beans into 1 1/2-inch lengths; leave pea pods whole or cut as desired. Place 1 tablespoon unsalted butter or olive oil for every 2 cups beans in a sauté pan or large, heavy skillet and heat over medium-high heat. Add the beans or peas and sauté until crisp-tender, 3 to 8 minutes. Season to taste with salt and pepper.

To stir-fry green beans or edible pod peas, trim and cut as for sautéing. Place a wok, large sauté pan, or large, heavy skillet over high heat. When the pan is hot, add about 1 tablespoon high-quality vegetable oil for every 2 cups beans and swirl to coat the pan. When the oil is hot but not yet smoking, add the beans or pea pods and stir-fry until coated with the oil, about 1 minute. Add about 2 tablespoons water, cover, and cook, stirring occasionally, until crisp-tender, 2 to 5 minutes. Season to taste with salt and pepper.

Each cup of beans makes 1 serving.

Dried Legumes

Nutritious beans, peas, and lentils are available dried year-round. When buying in packages or from bulk bins, look for plump, unshriveled specimens with skins that are brightly colored and free of any dusty haze that indicates old age. Whenever possible, purchase legumes that were harvested and dried during the most recent autumn. Avoid broken beans and examine closely for any tiny holes that disclose insect infestations. For even cooking, check to see that all legumes of a single type are about the same size.

Dried legumes will last indefinitely when placed in tightly sealed glass jars in a cool, dry place. Do not refrigerate, as dampness tends to toughen them. Dried legumes become drier with age, so the longer they are stored, the longer they will take to soften and cook. Older beans are more likely to fall apart during cooking and should only be used when they will be puréed, and not for dishes calling for whole beans.

Azuki beans *(Vigna angularis).* Native to Asia, these small red beans are usually sold by their common Japanese name, sometimes spelled *adzuki,* and are most frequently used in sweets. Slightly sweet flavor.

Black-eyed peas *(Vigna unguiculata* subspecies). These slightly kidney-shaped relatives of cowpeas (see Cowpeas entry) are marked with a single dark spot on the ridge of each bean. Very popular in the southern United States.

Butter beans *(Phaseolus lunatus).* Often called baby or small limas, these Peruvian native beans are popular in the Deep South. A speckled variety is dubbed Dixie speckled butter bean. Buttery texture and mellow flavor.

Cowpeas *(Vigna unguiculata).* Also known as cream, crowder, field, or lady peas, these small brown legumes are native to Central Africa and grown extensively in the southern United States. Subspecies include black-eyed peas (see Black-eyed peas entry) and the brown pigeon peas that are popular in the Caribbean and Latin America.

Cranberry beans *(Phaseolus vulgaris* varieties).* Descendants of kidney beans made their way from South America to Europe, where they became a favorite and were hybridized into Borlotti, French Horticultural, Rosecocos, Tongues of Fire, and other tasty varieties. Often called Roman beans, they, like most beans, lose their attractive mottling during cooking.

Fava beans *(Vicia faba).* These large, flat brown beans, with a dark line running along the divided seam, are known by a variety of names, including broad, field, horse, English, and European beans. A smaller, rounder relative, known as Egyptian beans, or *ful medames,* was a staple of ancient Egypt. Today fava beans are prized among Mediterranean cooks for their nutty flavor. Some people of Mediterranean descent inherit a blood disorder that may cause an allergic reaction to fava beans.

Garbanzo beans *(Cicer arientinum).* I prefer to call these large, roundish legumes by their Spanish name, but they are also known as chick-peas and sometimes sold by their Italian name, *ceci.* Colors include the common beige, as well as hard-to-find yellow, red, and black.

Kidney beans *(Phaseolus vulgaris).* The majority of hybrid beans available today trace their ancestry to the kidney-shaped beans that are native to tropical regions of America. They include every color known to the bean family and the characteristic kidney shape varies from pronounced to subtle.

The red kidney bean, often called Mexican bean, is probably the parent of a huge family of descendants and has been documented to have been cultivated since 5,000 B.C. Related red beans, the favorite of New Orleans cooks, and pink beans are both smaller and have a less pronounced kidney shape.

Black beans, sometimes sold as turtle beans, are extremely popular in the Southwest and Mexico because of their meaty texture and hearty, distinct flavor. Most authorities agree that these black-skinned beans with creamy white flesh do not require soaking.

Favorite white varieties include Great Northern, navy, and Italian *cannellini*, which the French call *haricots blancs,* as well as roundish marrow beans, tiny pea or California beans, and the roundish desert-grown Pueblo. Very pale green French *flageolets* are immature white kidney beans.

Not content with solid colors, kidney beans have evolved to include an interesting array of patterned beans. Some of my favorites include black-and-white Calypso, maroon-and-cream Jacob's Cattle and Anasazi, amber-splotched Steuben yellow-eyed, maroon-blotched red-eyed or Soldier, and the multicolored, multishaped Pebble, a hybrid from California's Phipps Ranch. Related subspecies include cranberry and pinto beans, which I've listed separately because of their distinct differences.

Lentils *(Lens culinaris).* One of the world's oldest food crops and native to India, lentils come in green, brown, or red and are sold either whole or split. Peeled red lentils, identified as *masoor dal* by Indian grocers and as Egyptian lentils in Middle Eastern markets, are actually salmon-colored legumes that turn dull yellow during cooking and hold their shape. Unpeeled red lentils

appear brownish on the outside due to the outer hull. Small Chinese or Persian brown lentils tend to fall apart during cooking. Green varieties include the readily available greenish brown lentils with mushy texture but good flavor, and the prized, meaty French variety, Le Puy, that holds its shape when cooked and is the best lentil for using in salads.

Lima beans *(Phaseolus limensis).* These large, flat beans are usually ivory colored with a hint of pale green and cook up with a creamy texture and slightly acidic flavor. Christmas lima is an old variety with burgundy mottling and chestnut flavor. Gigandes is a very large European hybrid.

Mung beans *(Vigna radiata).* Popular throughout Asia and probably native to Indonesia, these small roundish beans may be yellow, brown, black, or, in their most common form, dull green. They are sold whole, hulled, or split and identified as *moong* in Indian markets. In Asia, mung beans are used to make bean thread noodles, which turn translucent when cooked. These are popular beans for sprouting.

Peas *(Pisum sativum).* Green or yellow varieties of garden or English peas are sold either dried whole or split. Northern Europeans prefer yellow split peas, as do Indians, who call them *chana dal.* Quick cooking with a soft texture and sweet, earthy flavor.

Peanuts *(Arachis hypolgaea).* Although used more as a nut than a bean, the seedpods of this legume are set above ground, then buried by the plant to mature under the earth. Creamy texture and nutty flavor.

Pinto beans *(Phaseolus vulgaris var. humilis).* Close relatives of kidney beans, these oval-shaped legumes, sometimes called Mexican strawberries, come in shades of tan with a darker overall pattern that resembles the markings of the pinto horse. Heirloom types include Bayo from the southern bayou country and Buckskin grown in the western United States by Native Americans. New hybrids include Appaloosa and Rattlesnake. Mealy texture and rich flavor.

Runner beans *(Phaseolus coccineus).* Russet-colored varieties with dark mottling or flecks, called scarlet runners because of their brilliant flowers, are the most popular of this group of large thumbnail-shaped beans. White and black varieties are also available.

Soybeans *(Glycine max).* Native to China, but now widely grown in the United States, this is the only legume to contain all of the essential amino acids. Colors include black, brown, red, yellow, and green. Processed and fermented soybeans are the basis of many highly nutritious food products, including curd (tofu), paste *(miso),* beverages, soy sauce, and imitation meats.

Soaking and Cooking Dried Beans

Human digestive systems are incapable of breaking down the various complex sugars, including raffinose, stachyose, and verbascose, collectively known as alpha-galactrosides, found in beans. Bacteria living in the lower intestines, however, do break them down, resulting in the production of large amounts of several gases, including carbon dioxide, hydrogen, and methane.

Not all legumes are made the same. Greater amounts of the indigestible sugars are found in beans that are native to the Western Hemisphere—kidney, lima, navy, and pinto beans—than are present in the Asian natives—lentils, split peas, and *azuki* and mung beans. And today plant hybridizers are developing bean varieties genetically altered to lower the amount of indigestible sugars.

It seems that almost everyone has a solution to the problem of gases that result from eating beans. Mexican cooks throw a pungent herb, epazote, into simmering beans because it is thought to help counteract the gases' effects. Many food writers suggest changing the soaking water several times, then cooking in fresh water. According to authorities at the United States Department of Agriculture, however, this process does not aid in digestibility.

Soaking beans prior to cooking softens them and shortens their cooking time. The Quick Hot-Soak Method described on page 18 also makes the beans more digestible (see sidebar on page 17). Although beans can be cooked without soaking, they will take considerably longer to become tender. Lentils, split peas, black beans, and some new hybrid beans do not require soaking, however; check packages or ask sellers if in doubt.

Actual soaking time varies with variety; large types such as fava and lima beans need longer soaking periods than smaller beans. Generally, the longer beans are soaked, the shorter the cooking time and the more tender the result.

An exception to the general rules of soaking and cooking is the Italian lupine bean *(lupini)*. It contains a bitter alkaloid that must be leached out by soaking the beans in a salt-water brine for about a week with daily rinsing and fresh brine. Follow supplier's directions for these beans.

Although cooking beans in their soaking water conserves nutrients, disposing of the soaking water used in the Quick Hot-Soak Method, rinsing the beans, and cooking them in fresh liquid helps reduce the amount of insoluble sugars that cause gas (see adjacent sidebars). If you choose to soak black beans, however, you may want to cook them in the soaking liquid in order to retain more of their rich color pigments.

To preserve both color pigments and nutrients, avoid cooking legumes in too much liquid. Start by immersing soaked beans by no more than 1/2 inch, or unsoaked beans by no more than 2 inches, adding more liquid as needed to keep them covered.

Undercooked, crunchy beans are not only unappealing to chew, but also can be difficult to digest due to the presence of toxic lectin, which can cause stomachaches, diarrhea, or nausea. On the other hand, overcooked beans turn mushy. The trick is to cook beans until they are just tender and creamy yet still hold their shape; once they begin to split, they turn unpleasantly soft.

Cooking time varies with type of legume, length of storage, altitude, duration of soaking, and the hardness of the water. The older the bean, the longer it takes to cook. Since there are no labels to indicate age, estimating cooking time is a matter of guesswork. Always begin to taste before you think the beans will be done.

Pressure cookers reduce the cooking time by more than half due to the higher temperature that occurs inside the pressurized pot. They make it impossible to gauge when the beans are tender and to adjust the seasonings during cooking, however. To prevent overcooking, follow the manufacturer's directions, but shorten the time by a few minutes. If the beans are not yet done, finish cooking them conventionally.

Legumes absorb the flavors around them during cooking. Onions, garlic, celery, carrots, meat, and fresh and dried herbs may be added to the beans at the beginning. Acidic ingredients, such as tomatoes or tomato products, citrus juice, vinegar, or wine, interfere with the legumes' ability to bind with water, however, and will toughen bean skins and lengthen the cooking time. With some beans, acidic products prevent them from ever getting tender no matter how long they are cooked! Wait until the beans are done before adding these flavorings.

Cooking dried legumes with salt adds considerably to the cooking time, therefore the basic recipe (page 18) calls for seasoning with salt after the legumes are tender. If you wish to cook legumes in a liquid more flavorful than water, use unsalted stock, or use canned reduced-sodium broth and allow for extra cooking time.

Adding a bit of unsalted butter or vegetable oil helps prevent liquid from overflowing the pot during the boiling period. Some cooks advocate rubbing a little vegetable oil around the top edge of the cooking pot to accomplish this purpose.

Since cooking beans is time-consuming, you may wish to cook more dried beans than needed for a specific recipe and store the leftovers for another purpose. Cooked beans can be covered and refrigerated for up to 3 days, or they can be frozen for several months and then thawed before reheating. Liquid drained off cooked beans makes a delicious addition to soups or stews.

Food scientists today advocate dropping dried beans into rapidly boiling water and boiling for a few minutes, a procedure that tricks the seeds into beginning the process of growing into a new plant. The hot water softens the plant cell walls that protect the sugars, allowing them to leach into the water. The beans should then be removed from the heat, covered, and soaked for an hour or more. When the soaking water is discarded, about 85 percent of the insoluble sugars are drained off. Of course, some nutrients, as well as color pigment, will also go down the drain, but if you are bothered by intestinal gases from eating beans, it will be worth the slight sacrifice.

Another option is to use Beano, a liquid food additive that contains an enzyme that breaks down the sugars before the intestinal bacteria have a chance to go to work. Many swear that it greatly reduces or eliminates gas problems.

Perhaps the easiest solution is simply to eat more beans. It is believed by some that when one eats beans on a regular basis, the problem of gas lessens over time.

Cooked Dried Beans

Dried beans, peas, or lentils
Unsalted vegetable, poultry, or meat stock
   (optional)
1 tablespoon unsalted butter or vegetable oil
   (optional)
Salt (optional)
Freshly ground black pepper (optional)

This basic recipe works for cooking any type of dried bean or other legume. Except for salt and pepper added at the end, I've omitted seasonings, resulting in a pot of beans that can be used in a variety of dishes. For more flavorful beans to be served on their own, select one of the well-seasoned variations that follow.

Spread the beans, peas, or lentils out on a tray or flat surface and carefully pick over by hand to remove any foreign bits or imperfect legumes. Place the legumes in a colander or sieve and rinse well under cold running water to remove the dust accumulated during drying and storing.

If using split peas, lentils, black beans, and some new varieties of beans that do not require soaking (see page 16), you may skip the next three paragraphs and proceed with cooking. If using other legumes, soak by one of the following methods.

Quick Hot-Soak Method. In a heavy-bottomed pot, bring enough water to cover the legumes later by about 3 inches to a boil over high heat. Add the picked over and rinsed legumes, return the water to a boil, and boil for 3 to 5 minutes. Remove from the heat, cover, and let stand for 1 hour or longer; extra soaking time will result in shorter cooking time. If soaking longer than 2 hours, refrigerate after cooling to room temperature to prevent fermentation.

Long Cold-Soak Method. Place the legumes in a large bowl and add tepid water to cover by about 3 inches. Let stand for several hours or, preferably, overnight. When soaking during hot weather, refrigerate to prevent fermentation.

Drain the soaked legumes in a colander or sieve, reserving the liquid for cooking if desired (see page 16). Rinse the beans under cold running water and drain again. If using whole fava beans, peel off and discard the layer of skin from each bean.

Transfer the drained legumes to a large, heavy-bottomed saucepan or other pot. If the legumes were soaked, add enough stock, water, or reserved soaking liquid to cover by about 1/2 inch and stir well. If the legumes were not soaked, add enough liquid to cover by about 2 inches and stir well. Avoid filling the pot more than three-quarters full. Add butter or oil, if desired, to reduce the amount of foaming and help prevent liquid from boiling over. Place over medium-high heat and bring to a boil. Using a wire skimmer or slotted utensil, remove any foam that comes to the surface.

If cooking lentils or split peas, immediately reduce the heat to achieve a simmer and cover partially.

If cooking beans, boil for 10 minutes, then reduce the heat to achieve a simmer and cover partially.

Simmer, stirring occasionally, until the lentils, peas, or beans are tender but still hold their shape and have absorbed most of the water, about 20 minutes for lentils or split peas, or 20 minutes to 2 hours for most beans and whole peas. Large bean varieties, those stored for long periods, or beans cooked in salted stock or broth may take even longer. Test frequently for doneness and taste several beans for consistency. Add a little liquid as required if the legumes get too dry, but use as little liquid as possible, keeping the beans only slightly submerged. Avoid overcooking at any point to prevent the beans from becoming mushy.

If serving the legumes on their own, season to taste with salt and pepper. (To thicken the bean liquid, if desired, remove and mash about 1/2 cup of the beans, then stir them back into the pot.)

If using the beans in the following variations (pages 21-23) or in recipes, season as directed.

Each cup dried legumes makes 2 to 3 cups cooked legumes, depending upon variety, enough for 2 or 3 servings.

USING CANNED BEANS

When cooking time is limited, canned beans are an acceptable alternative for many dishes. Just bear in mind that only a few varieties are available canned, and these are often much saltier, less flavorful, and generally more expensive than their dried counterparts.

Drain and rinse canned beans to refresh their flavor before using them.

A World of Well-Seasoned Beans

Here are a few of my favorite American regional and international bean dishes. Use the preceding basic recipe as a guide and serve them with the suggested grain (cooked as directed on pages 31-35), or use them as directed in other recipes in this book. For Indian-style beans, follow the recipe for *dal* on page 64. For Italian-style beans, see the recipe for Tuscan White Beans in *James McNair Cooks Italian.*

Although I've chosen to stick with the traditional additions of meat for flavoring these international styles, any of them that use meat can be turned into vegetarian beans by omitting the meat, cooking the onions or other vegetables in a little olive oil or vegetable oil, and using vegetable stock (for optimum flavor) or water.

Each of these recipes can be transformed into a flavorful soup by increasing the amount of liquid to cover the beans to about 3 inches and adding enough liquid during cooking to maintain a "soupy" consistency. For a creamy soup, simmer until the beans begin to fall apart, then purée in a food processor or blender and, if desired, put through a food mill, sieve, or conical *chinois* to remove the skins.

Brazilian-Style Beans

Serve with long-grain white rice.

2 cups dried black beans
8 ounces bacon, chopped
1 cup finely chopped yellow onion
1 teaspoon minced garlic
1 teaspoon ground cumin
2 bay leaves
1 tablespoon brown sugar
1/2 cup tomato purée
Salt
Freshly ground black pepper
3 tablespoons chopped fresh cilantro (coriander)
2 tablespoons freshly squeezed lime juice, or to taste

Pick over and rinse the beans as directed in the basic recipe and set aside.

In a large, heavy pot, cook the bacon over medium heat until the fat is rendered. Add the onion and sauté until soft, about 5 minutes. Add the beans, garlic, cumin, bay leaves, brown sugar, and enough water to cover by about 2 inches. Cook as directed in the basic recipe until the beans are tender.

Add the tomato purée and salt and pepper to taste and simmer until the flavors are well blended, about 20 minutes. Just before serving, stir in the cilantro and lime juice.

Makes 6 servings.

French-Style Beans

Serve with couscous or pearled barley.

2 cups dried white beans, preferably *flageolets*
2 tablespoons fat from duck or goose confit
2 cups finely chopped leek, including green portion
1 tablespoon minced garlic
About 2 quarts unsalted poultry or vegetable stock (optional)
2 cups peeled and chopped tomato
1/2 cup minced fresh parsley
6 ounces chopped duck or goose confit
Salt
Freshly ground black pepper

Clean and soak the beans as directed in the basic recipe.

Drain the beans and transfer to a large, heavy pot. Stir in the confit fat, leek, garlic, and enough stock or water to cover by 1/2 inch. Cook as directed in the basic recipe until the beans are tender.

Add the tomato, parsley, chopped confit, and salt and pepper to taste and simmer until the flavors are well blended, about 20 minutes.

Makes 6 servings.

Mexicali Beans

Serve with long-grain white rice or flour or corn tortillas.

2 cups dried black, pink, pinto, kidney, or similar beans
1 tablespoon cumin seed
1 tablespoon dried oregano
2 tablespoons freshly ground dried chile, preferably *ancho* or *pasilla*
2 tablespoons olive oil
2 cups chopped yellow onion
2 teaspoons minced garlic
Salt
Freshly ground black pepper

Cook the beans until tender as directed in the basic recipe.

In a skillet, combine the cumin, oregano, and chile. Place over medium heat and toast, stirring or shaking the pan frequently, until fragrant, about 5 minutes; do not allow to burn. Transfer to a spice grinder or heavy mortar with a pestle and grind to a powder. Set aside.

In a heavy skillet or saucepan, heat the olive oil over medium-high heat. Add the onion and sauté until golden and very soft, about 8 minutes. Add the garlic and sauté about 1 minute longer. Stir into the beans. Add the spice mixture and season to taste with salt and pepper. Simmer until the flavors are well blended, about 20 minutes.

Makes 6 servings.

New Orleans-Style Beans

Serve with long-grain white rice.

2 cups dried small red beans
12 ounces smoked pork, cubed
12 ounces smoked pork sausage, sliced about 3/4 inch thick
2 cups chopped yellow onion
1 cup chopped celery
1 cup chopped green sweet pepper
1 tablespoon minced garlic
1/4 cup minced fresh parsley
2 teaspoons dried thyme
1 teaspoon dried oregano
3 bay leaves
About 2 quarts unsalted chicken or vegetable stock (optional)
Salt
Freshly ground black pepper
Ground cayenne pepper
Bottled Louisiana-style hot sauce

Clean and soak the beans as directed in the basic recipe.

In a large, heavy pot, combine the pork and sausage, place over medium-high heat, and sauté until the fat is rendered. Add the onion, celery, and sweet pepper and sauté until soft and golden, about 8 minutes. Add the garlic and sauté about 1 minute longer.

Drain the beans and stir them into the pot. Add the herbs and enough stock or water to cover by 1/2 inch. Cook as directed in the basic recipe until the beans are tender. Season to taste with salt, peppers, and hot sauce.

Makes 6 servings.

North African-Style Beans

Serve with couscous or wheat berries.

2 cups dried Egyptian fava (*ful medames*) or garbanzo beans
3 tablespoons olive oil
3 cups chopped yellow onion
1 cup chopped carrot
1 teaspoon minced garlic
1 cinnamon stick, 3 inches long
3 whole cloves
1/2 teaspoon saffron threads
6 fresh cilantro (coriander) sprigs
6 fresh flat-leaf parsley sprigs
About 2 quarts unsalted chicken or vegetable stock (optional)
1 cup peeled and chopped tomato
Salt
Freshly ground black pepper

Clean and soak the beans as directed in the basic recipe.

In a large, heavy pot, heat the oil over medium-high heat. Add the onion and carrot and sauté until the vegetables are soft, about 5 minutes. Add the garlic, cinnamon, cloves, and saffron and sauté about 1 minute longer.

Drain the beans and stir them into the pot. Add the cilantro and parsley sprigs and enough stock or water to cover by 1/2 inch. Cook as directed in the basic recipe until the beans are tender.

Stir in the tomato and salt and pepper to taste and simmer until the flavors are well blended, about 20 minutes.

Makes 6 servings.

Southern-Style Beans

Serve with your favorite cornbread or see *James McNair's Corn Cookbook* for a variety of cornbreads.

2 cups dried lima beans or black-eyed peas
3 tablespoons bacon drippings or vegetable oil
3 cups sliced yellow onion
1 pound smoked pork, cubed
2 bay leaves
About 2 quarts unsalted chicken or meat stock (optional)
Salt
Freshly ground black pepper

Clean and soak the beans as directed in the basic recipe.

In a large, heavy pot, heat the bacon drippings or oil over medium-high heat. Add the onion and sauté until soft, about 5 minutes.

Drain the beans and stir them into the pot. Add the pork, bay leaves, and enough stock or water to cover by 1/2 inch. Cook as directed in the basic recipe until the beans are tender. Season to taste with salt and pepper.

Makes 6 servings.

Southwestern-Style Beans

Serve with tortillas or hominy.

2 cups dried black beans
4 ounces bacon, chopped
1 cup chopped yellow onion
1 cup chopped celery
1/2 cup chopped carrot
1 tablespoon chopped fresh jalapeño or other hot chile
1 bay leaf
4 teaspoons minced or pressed garlic
1 tablespoon chili powder
2 teaspoons ground cumin
Ground cayenne pepper
Freshly ground black pepper
About 2 quarts unsalted chicken or vegetable stock (optional)
Salt

Pick over and rinse the beans as directed in the basic recipe.

In a large, heavy pot, cook the bacon over medium heat until the fat is rendered. Add the onion, celery, carrot, fresh chile, and bay leaf and sauté until the vegetables are soft and golden, about 8 minutes. Add the garlic, chili powder, cumin, and ground peppers to taste and sauté about 2 minutes. Stir in the beans and enough stock or water to cover by about 2 inches. Cook as directed in the basic recipe until the beans are tender. Season to taste with salt.

Makes 6 servings.

Spanish-Style Beans

Serve with short-grain white rice.

2 cups dried lima or fava beans
3 tablespoons olive oil
4 cups sliced yellow onion
1 cup chopped leek, including green portion
1 cup chopped carrot
3 tablespoons minced garlic
1 pound chorizo sausages, casings discarded, sliced
2 bay leaves
1 tablespoon paprika
About 2 quarts unsalted chicken or meat stock (optional)
Salt
Freshly ground black pepper

Clean and soak the beans as directed in the basic recipe.

In a large, heavy pot, heat the oil over low heat. Add the onion, leek, carrot, and garlic and cook, stirring frequently, until the vegetables are almost caramelized, about 45 minutes.

Drain the beans and stir them into the pot. Add the sausage, bay leaves, paprika, and enough stock or water to cover by 1/2 inch. Cook as directed in the basic recipe until the beans are tender. Season to taste with salt and pepper.

Makes 6 servings.

American Baked Beans

No all-American celebration would be complete without a side dish of baked beans. This generic recipe illustrates the method for baking, while the variations add typical regional flourishes. For vegetarian beans, substitute 2 tablespoons high-quality vegetable oil for the seasoning meat.

Choose one type of bean, a packaged mixture of bean varieties that have been selected because they share similar cooking times, or a combination of separately cooked beans.

If using dried beans, cook until tender as directed in the basic recipe on page 18 and set aside; do not season. If using canned beans, reserve for later use.

Preheat an oven to 275° F.

In a saucepan, bring about 4 cups water to a boil over high heat. Add the salt pork and boil for 5 minutes. Drain the pork, rinse under cold running water, transfer to a work surface, and cut into small dice.

Drain the beans, reserving the liquid, and transfer 8 cups to a mixing bowl (cover and refrigerate or freeze any remaining beans for another purpose). Measure the liquid, adding water if necessary, to equal 3 cups and stir into the beans. Add the pork, onion, molasses, brown sugar, catsup, mustard, salt, and pepper and mix well. Transfer the mixture to a lightly greased bean pot or 3-quart baking dish, cover tightly with a lid or aluminum foil, and bake, stirring occasionally, until very tender and well flavored, about 5 hours. If the beans get dry before they are ready, add a little more of the bean liquid or water.

Makes 8 servings.

4 cups dried beans, or 8 cups canned beans
8 ounces salt pork, trimmed of rind
3 cups chopped yellow onion
1/2 cup unsulphured light molasses
1/2 cup packed brown sugar
1/2 cup catsup
2 tablespoons dry mustard or prepared Dijon mustard
4 teaspoons salt, or to taste
1 teaspoon freshly ground black pepper, or to taste

BAKED BEAN VARIATIONS

Baked Beans and Rice. Bake the beans according to the basic recipe or any of the following variations. Meanwhile, cook 2 cups brown rice or a mixture of wild and brown rices such as Lundberg Wild Blend. Combine the cooked rice and the baked beans, transfer to a greased 9-by-13-inch baking dish, and bake in a 350° F oven until well flavored and bubbly, about 45 minutes. Just before serving, shower the top with minced fresh chives or green onion tops to garnish.

Barbecued Baked Beans. Omit the catsup. Add 1 cup high-quality barbecue sauce.

Boston Baked Beans. Use small white beans, such as navy or Great Northern. Omit the catsup.

Hawaiian Baked Beans. Use navy beans. Omit the salt pork, molasses, catsup, mustard, and salt. Increase the brown sugar to 1 cup. Add 2 cups cubed Spam (about 12 ounces), 2 cups drained canned pineapple chunks (reserve juice and use as part of the liquid stirred into the beans), 1 cup soy sauce, 1/4 cup finely chopped fresh ginger, and 4 teaspoons minced or pressed garlic.

New England Baked Beans. Use yellow-eyed beans or small white beans, such as navy or Great Northern. Omit the brown sugar and molasses. Add 1 cup packed maple sugar or pure maple syrup.

Southern Baked Beans. Use kidney, lima, or navy beans. Use the salt pork or 8 ounces chopped bacon or baked ham. Increase the catsup to 1 cup and add 2 tablespoons Worcestershire sauce.

Western Baked Beans. Use black, red kidney, pinto, or similar beans. Add 1/4 cup chopped fresh hot chile such as jalapeño or serrano, or to taste, and 2 tablespoons Worcestershire sauce.

Grains

With the exception of sweet corn, all grains are used in their dried form.

Fresh sweet corn should be cooked as soon as possible after it is picked, preferably right from the garden or farm. In markets, avoid ears that feel warm to the touch, as they will probably cook up tough because heat, like time, activates starch conversion. If corn can't be cooked the day it is picked, choose Supersweet varieties, which hold their sugar content longer. Stems and husks should be pale green, not straw colored, and a bit moist. Avoid ears with brown stems. Store in the refrigerator for up to 3 days for Supersweet corn.

Since the germ oil in dried grains can quickly turn rancid, it is a good idea to purchase them from a store where a quick turnover is likely. Look for even color and plump, unshriveled kernels. Avoid grains with musty or rancid odors.

Grains will last indefinitely when placed in tightly sealed glass jars in a dark place that is cool and dry. In hot climates, refrigerate whole grains (except polished grains such as white rice and pearled barley) in airtight containers. Always smell grains for rancidity before using. Harmless yet annoying grain weevils may develop even in properly stored grains.

Stored whole grains can be ground into meal or flour as needed or purchased in a number of preground or cut forms.

Products made from processed grains include cereals, pastas, and breads.

Amaranth *(Amaranthus hybridus* and *A. caudatus).* This tiny powerhouse of protein and vitamins has been cultivated in Asia for centuries. The Aztecs of Mexico grew amaranth not only as a major food crop, but also for blending with human blood in ritual sacrifices, a practice that revolted the conquering "Christians" and resulted in the near annihilation of the grain in the West. Fortunately, the little golden, purple, or black grain survived and is currently enjoying renewed popularity. Available forms include whole and flour.

Barley *(Hordeum vulgare).* Barley is native to the temperate zones of the Northern Hemisphere. As unhulled whole grain barley is virtually impossible to tenderize no matter how long it cooks, purchase hulled grains or polished grains, known as pearled barley. Available forms include whole, rolled, and grits.

Buckwheat *(Fagopyrum esculentum).* When the grains from this native European and Asian grass are roasted, they become highly aromatic and are usually sold under the name kasha, taken from the Russian. Unroasted and roasted available forms include whole (groats), cracked, grits, and flour.

Bulgur. A popular food of the Middle East and eastern Europe, bulgur is actually whole wheat that has been hulled, cleaned, steamed, and dried. It is sold whole or cracked into fine to coarse granules and ranges from dark to light, depending upon the type of wheat used. Since the steaming precooks the grain, bulgur needs only to be reconstituted in boiling water to soften. When buying, be sure to notice the difference between bulgur and cracked wheat (see Wheat entry), which must be cooked before using.

Corn *(Zea mays).* These giant grass stalks originated in Central America and produce ears of grains in yellow, white, blue, red, and black. The only grain that we enjoy fresh is sweet corn or sugar corn *(Z. mays* var. *saccharta),* which contains much more sugar than any other corn.

Whole dried yellow or white kernels of field or dent corn *(Z. mays* var. *indentata)* and blue or red Indian or flint corn *(Z. mays* var. *indurata)* must be treated with lime or lye to remove the hulls and partially tenderize the kernels, a process that turns the corn into what we call hominy in most of North America, *posole* in the Southwest, and *nixtamal* in Mexico. Available forms of hominy include dried whole, canned, and grits. Available forms of dried corn include whole, meal, and flour.

Couscous. Made from hard durum wheat, or semolina, this "pasta" from North Africa resembles tiny round grains and is used like grains.

Job's tears *(Coix Lacryma-Jobi).* Many food writers classify this large grain as a type of barley. In fact, it is a native grass of Southeast Asia. The teardrop shape inspired the English common name. It may also be sold as river grain or by one of its Japanese names, *yobe* or *hato mugi.* Available in whole form.

Millet *(Panicum miliaceum).* A native Asian grass that produces a round, golden grain, millet is now widely cultivated in hot, dry climates throughout the world. It is easily digested and highly adaptable for use in many dishes. Available forms include whole, meal, and flour.

Oats *(Avena sativa).* Native to Mediterranean Europe and North Africa, oats are a centuries-old staple of northern Europe. Available forms include whole (groats), rolled, steel-cut (Scottish oats), grits, and flour.

Quinoa *(Chenopodium quinoa).* This ancient staple of the Incas, native to the Andes and pronounced KEEN-wah, has enjoyed increased popularity in recent years. Although botanically an herb, its minuscule fruits are used as a grain and contain twice the protein found in most grains. An insect repellent, saponin, is formed by the plant and must be washed off before cooking to prevent bitterness. Even packages labeled prewashed should be thoroughly rinsed to be certain all traces are removed. Available forms include whole and flour.

Rice *(Oryza sativa indica* and *O. s. japonica).* Most of the rice eaten in the world is harvested from descendants of two varieties. *Japonica* rice, known as glutinous, sweet, sticky, or waxy rice, is the daily grain of preference in Laos and northeast Thailand, and is used in sweets or snacks throughout Asia.

North Americans are more familiar with *indica* varieties, native to India, that are divided into classes according to the length of their grains—short, medium, and long. Long-grain varieties yield fluffy grains that remain separate after cooking and are preferred by most Americans and Asians; extremely flavorful varieties include jasmine from Southeast Asia and *basmati* from India and Iran, also grown in Texas as Texmati. Medium- and short-grain varieties stick together after cooking.

Medium-grain rice is preferred by Japanese and Korean cooks. Short-grain varieties include Italian Arborio and American-grown pearl.

Rices may be purchased brown (bran and germ intact) or white (polished). Available forms include whole and flour.

Rye *(Secale cereale).* Although native to the mountains of Southeast Asia, rye is now cultivated in Europe. The flavor of cooked rye is quite different from the distinctive sour taste associated with rye breads, which comes from the starters used. Available forms include whole (berries), rolled, grits, meal, and flour.

Teff *(Eragrostis Tef).* Extremely tiny and packed with nutrition, this ancient white, red, or brown grain from Ethiopia is becoming readily obtainable in North America. Available forms include whole and flour.

Triticale *(Triticum* x *Secale).* This botanical cross between rye and wheat (pronounced trit-i-KAY-lee) is another highly nutritious food that deserves to be added to our grain pantry. Although difficult to locate, even in natural-foods stores, available forms include whole (berries), rolled, cracked, and flour.

GRAIN TERMINOLOGY

Wheat *(Triticum* species). Whole-grain wheat is a delicious alternative to rice or other grains. Native to Southeast Asia and the Mediterranean area, wheat is a major crop of North America. Two ancient types, spelt and kamut, are enjoying newfound popularity; both possess a nutty flavor and are often tolerated by those with allergies to other wheats. Colors range from white to red and grains may be soft or hard (durum). Available forms include whole (berries), rolled, cracked, and flour. Keep in mind that cracked wheat is not the same as bulgur (see entry), which may also be labeled as precooked cracked wheat.

Wild rice *(Zizania aquatica).* Technically, what we call wild rice is not a rice, but the elongated black seeds of a wild aquatic grass found mainly in the north-central United States and in Canada. The grain is expensive due to the short season, limited supply, and hand gathering and thrashing. Available in whole form.

Berries. Whole grains, usually husked or hulled. Term normally used for rye, triticale, or wheat.

Bran. The fibrous layer between the inedible husk and the germ of a grain kernel.

Cracked. Whole grains that have been broken into granules of various sizes.

Endosperm. Heart of a grain kernel after removing the layers of husk, bran, and germ.

Flour. Very finely ground grain.

Germ. Nutritious layer between the bran and endosperm of a kernel of grain.

Grains. The edible seeds, or kernels, of cereal grasses.

Grits. Coarsely ground grain. Most often used with hominy corn.

Groats. Either whole hulled grains or hulled grains that have been cracked. Term normally used with buckwheat and oats.

Husk. Inedible outer layer of a grain kernel. Also called chaff or hull.

Meal. Coarsely to finely ground grain. Neither as coarsely ground as grits nor as finely ground as flour.

Pearled. Hulled and polished.

Puffed. Whole grain puffed under pressure.

Rolled. Grain flakes that have been steamed, then flattened between rollers.

Stone-ground. Meal or flour ground with an old-fashioned milling stone.

Cooked Whole Grains

This basic recipe can be used for all whole grains. Many grains also come in cracked, ground (grits), or flaked forms and are usually cooked as a breakfast cereal; follow package directions for cooking these forms.

Rinsing the grains before cooking is advised for washing off the dust that collects from harvesting, drying, and storing. Be certain to wash quinoa thoroughly to remove the coating of saponin, a natural insect repellant secreted by the plant.

Dried grains can be cooked without soaking, although soaking whole hominy, oats, triticale, and wheat will decrease their cooking times by as much as one-half. Rice may also be soaked for more even cooking.

The exact amount of liquid and cooking time may vary with the size of grain variety, length of storage, altitude, and personal preference. Initially, use the measurements given, then adjust the amount of liquid and/or cooking time if necessary for future pots of the same grain.

When cooking amaranth, hominy, rye, triticale, or wheat, add salt after the grain is cooked, as salt prevents the absorption of liquid and causes these grains to toughen before they are tender. For added flavor, however, these grains can be cooked in unsalted vegetable, poultry, or meat stock instead of water. Other grains can be cooked in salted water, canned reduced-sodium broth, or salted stock.

Grains cooked in water can be eaten immediately with milk or yogurt, sweeteners, or fruits as a breakfast cereal or snack. Cooked whole grains may be served as a side dish, plain or with a savory sauce. Or use them in stuffings, pilafs, puddings, casseroles, and other dishes. Cooked whole amaranth and teff form a sticky mass similar to cooked cornmeal or polenta and are not suitable for use in recipes that call for drier, separated grains, such as salads; use them as cereals or as you would polenta in any favorite recipe.

Cooked grains can be successfully refrigerated in covered containers for up to 1 week; reheat briefly in a microwave or with a little liquid in a saucepan over low heat.

→

USING A RICE COOKER

If you cook rice frequently and have room for another kitchen appliance, you might invest in an electric rice cooker, which consistently produces perfect rice. It also does a fine job with buckwheat, millet, and quinoa. Use the amount of liquid specified in the chart on page 33 and allow the recommended resting time after the cooker shuts itself off.

Whole grains
Water, stock, or canned broth (see recipe introduction for type and use and see accompanying chart for amount)
Salt (optional; see recipe introduction)
Unsalted butter or high-quality vegetable oil (optional)

Spread the grains out on a tray or other flat surface and carefully pick over by hand to remove any foreign bits or imperfect grains. Place in a bowl, add cold water to cover, and stir vigorously with your fingertips to wash, then drain off the water through a fine-mesh sieve. Repeat if necessary until the water is clear.

Soak hominy, oats, triticale, wheat, or rice if desired (see recipe introduction). To soak, place the washed grains in a bowl, add cold water to cover, and set aside to soak, about 1 hour for rice, or overnight for other grains. Drain just before cooking. If desired, reserve the soaking water to use as part of the cooking liquid.

In a heavy saucepan, combine the grain with the water, stock, or broth and add salt to taste (if using). Place over medium-high heat and bring to a boil. Stir the grain, cover tightly, reduce the heat to very low, and simmer until the liquid is absorbed and grains are tender (some grains will remain a bit chewy when fully cooked); see accompanying chart for approximate cooking times. If grains that require a long cooking time become too dry toward the end of cooking, add a little water.

If cooking amaranth or teff, remove from the heat, stir well, and serve or use immediately, or pour into a dish to cool completely and use as you would polenta. If cooking other grains, remove from the heat, remove the lid, cover the pot with paper toweling, replace the lid, and let rest for the time indicated.

Alternatively, for fluffier, separated grains, bring the liquid to a boil. Meanwhile, in a heavy-bottomed saucepan, heat 2 teaspoons butter or oil per cup of grain over medium heat, add the grain, and cook, stirring or shaking continuously, until the grain is fragrant and well coated with the butter or oil, about 2 minutes. Stir in the boiling liquid and salt to taste (if using), cover tightly, reduce the heat to very low, and proceed with cooking as above.

Drain off any liquid that remains in the pan after the grains are tender and rested. Season to taste with salt if desired. Using a fork, lift the grain from the bottom to fluff without breaking the tender grains. Serve or use as directed in recipes.

Each cup cooked whole grain makes 1 serving.

Cooking Whole Grains by the Absorption Method

GRAIN *Per 1 cup*	LIQUID *Water, stock, or broth*	COOK TIME *Approximate, after adjusting boil to simmer*	REST TIME *Off the heat*	YIELD *Approximate*
AMARANTH	3 cups (unsalted)	25 minutes	None	2 1/2 cups
BARLEY:				
Hulled	3 cups	1 hour	10 minutes	3 1/2 cups
Pearled	3 cups	30 minutes	10 minutes	3 1/2 cups
BUCKWHEAT	2 cups	15 minutes	5 minutes	3 cups
HOMINY	4 cups (unsalted)	3 hours	10 minutes	3 cups
JOB'S TEARS	3 cups	40 minutes	10 minutes	2 1/2 cups
MILLET	2 cups	15 minutes	10 minutes	4 cups
OATS	3 cups	1 hour	10 minutes	2 1/2 cups
QUINOA	2 cups	12 to 15 minutes	5 minutes	3 1/2 cups
RICE:				
White	1 1/2 cups*	17 minutes	10 minutes	3 cups
Brown	2 cups	45 minutes	10 minutes	3 to 4 cups
RYE	3 cups (unsalted)	1 hour	10 minutes	3 cups
TEFF	3 cups	20 minutes	None	3 cups
TRITICALE	3 cups (unsalted)	1 1/2 hours	5 minutes	3 cups
WHEAT	3 1/2 cups (unsalted)	1 1/2 hours	10 minutes	3 cups
WILD RICE	4 cups	45 minutes	5 minutes	4 cups

If cooking more than 2 cups white rice, add only 1 cup liquid for each additional cup of grain.

Following are a few grains or grain products that require a cooking technique other than the preceding absorption method or that can be cooked in ways in addition to that method.

Popped Amaranth

This ancient grain will pop much in the same way as popcorn. Mexican cooks mix popped amaranth with honey to make *alegria*, and in India it is stirred into milk to make *laddos* for feast days. Use it as a garnish or serve as a nutritious snack.

Amaranth
Salt

Heat a deep, heavy-bottomed saucepan or wok over high heat until almost smoking. Add 1 tablespoon raw amaranth at a time and quickly place a screen over the pan to keep the grains from escaping. Shake the pan until the grains stop popping, about 2 minutes. Pour into a bowl and season to taste with salt.

Each tablespoon amaranth yields about 1/2 cup popped grain.

Bulgur

Bulgur requires no cooking. It need only be reconstituted in hot liquid before using in recipes.

Bulgur
Boiling vegetable, poultry, or meat stock; canned reduced-sodium broth; or water

Wash and drain the bulgur as directed in the basic recipe on page 31 and place in a bowl.

Add 3 cups boiling liquid per 1 cup bulgur used, stir well, and let stand until the grains are tender yet firm to the bite, about 15 minutes for fine granules, about 30 minutes for medium granules, about 1 hour for coarse granules, or about 1 1/2 hours for whole grains.

Line a sieve or colander with dampened cheesecloth. Drain the bulgur through the cheesecloth, then gather the cheesecloth into a bag and squeeze out excess liquid. Transfer the bulgur to a bowl and, using a fork, lift the bulgur from the bottom to fluff without breaking the tender grains. Use as directed in recipes.

Each cup uncooked bulgur makes about 3 cups cooked.

Couscous

Traditionally, couscous is alternately steamed and dried several times until very airy in a special two-tiered pot (*couscousière*) over a simmering stew or salted water.

Most of the couscous available in North America is the parboiled quick-cooking variety and merely needs to be soaked in boiling liquid until softened. Although it lacks the airy texture and flavor of authentic couscous, it makes a perfectly reasonable substitute. It tastes best when reconstituted in stock or broth.

The following method differs slightly from package directions.

Quick-cooking couscous
Boiling vegetable, poultry, or meat stock; canned reduced-sodium broth; or water
Unsalted butter
Salt
Freshly ground black pepper

Wash and drain the couscous as directed in the basic recipe on page 31 and place in a shallow bowl.

In a saucepan, combine 1 1/2 cups stock, broth, or water and 1 tablespoon butter per 1 cup couscous used. Place over medium-high heat and bring to a boil. Pour over the couscous, add salt and pepper to taste, and quickly stir to mix well. Cover the couscous with a lid or aluminum foil and let stand for 10 minutes to absorb the liquid.

Using a fork, lift the couscous from the bottom to fluff without breaking the tender granules. Serve or use as directed in recipes.

Each cup uncooked couscous makes about 3 cups cooked, enough for 3 servings.

Kasha

Roasted buckwheat, which is commonly known as kasha, is usually cooked according to this traditional eastern European method.

Cooked kasha may be served on its own as a side dish or combined with cooked bow-tie or butterfly pasta *(farfalle)* for the classic Jewish dish *kasha varnishkes.*

Kasha, whole (groats) or cracked
Vegetable, poultry, or meat stock; canned reduced-sodium broth; or salted water
1 egg per 1 cup of kasha used, lightly beaten
Salt

Wash and drain the kasha as directed in the basic recipe on page 31.

In a saucepan, pour in 2 cups stock, broth, or water per 1 cup of kasha used, place over high heat, and bring to a boil.

Meanwhile, in a nonstick saucepan, combine the drained kasha and the egg(s). Place over medium heat and cook, stirring constantly with a wooden spoon, until the grains are separated and coated with egg, 2 to 3 minutes. Stir in the boiling liquid, cover tightly, reduce the heat to very low, and simmer until the liquid is absorbed and the kasha is tender, about 5 minutes for fine granules, about 8 minutes for medium granules, about 12 minutes for coarse granules, or about 15 minutes for whole groats. Season to taste with salt. Using a fork, lift the kasha from the bottom to fluff without breaking the tender grains. Serve or use as directed in recipes.

Each cup uncooked kasha makes about 3 cups cooked, enough for 3 servings.

Sunshine Granola

Most commercial granolas contain added oil or butter and are a bit too sweet. This low-fat version lets the taste of the grains shine through. If you prefer a richer blend, mix the grains with about 1/2 cup high-quality vegetable oil or melted butter before toasting. For a sweeter product, add about 1/4 cup honey to the raw mixture. If desired, stir 1 cup raisins, dried cherries or cranberries, chopped dates or other dried fruit, or a combination of dried fruits into the slightly cooled granola.

4 cups rolled barley, oats, rye, triticale, or wheat, or a combination
1/2 cup raw sunflower seeds
1/2 cup chopped raw or blanched almonds or other nuts or peanuts
1 tablespoon grated or minced fresh orange zest
1 cup thawed frozen orange juice concentrate

Preheat an oven to 300° F.

In a large mixing bowl, combine the rolled grain(s), sunflower seeds, nuts or peanuts, and orange zest and mix well. Add the orange juice concentrate and mix thoroughly. Spread the mixture in a large, shallow roasting pan and bake, stirring occasionally, until dry and toasted, about 45 minutes.

Pour into a large mixing bowl to cool, stirring occasionally. When completely cooled, store in an airtight container.

Makes 5 cups, enough for 5 servings.

COMBINATIONS

Bean Dips and Spreads
with Chips or Breads

**CHILI BEAN DIP OR SPREAD
WITH TORTILLAS**

2 cups Mexicali Beans (page 22)

2 tablespoons tomato paste

1½ teaspoons minced canned *chipotle* chile
   in *adobo* sauce, or to taste

1½ teaspoons *adobo* sauce from canned
   chiles, or to taste

Fresh cilantro (coriander) for garnish

Corn tortilla chips for dipping or warm corn
   tortillas for spreading

**ROASTED GARLIC AND BEAN
SPREAD WITH CRUSTY BREAD**

1 cup dried small white beans, such as
   cannellini or *flageolets*, or 2 cups canned
   small white beans

2 or 3 whole garlic heads

Olive oil, preferably extra-virgin

Salt

Freshly ground black pepper

Fresh flat-leaf parsley for garnish

Sliced whole-grain French- or Italian-style
   bread

These recipes illustrate two versions of puréed beans that may be used for dipping corn chips or spreading onto whole-grain breads. Use the techniques with any cooked beans and favorite seasonings to create your own flavorful recipes.

The photograph shows the Mediterranean-inspired Roasted Garlic and Bean Spread.

To make the Chili Bean Dip, cook the beans as directed. Drain the beans and transfer to a food processor or blender. Add the tomato paste, chile, and *adobo* sauce and blend until smooth. Transfer to a bowl, garnish with cilantro, and serve at room temperature with corn chips or tortillas.

To make the Roasted Garlic and Bean Spread, if using dried beans, cook the beans as directed on page 18 and set aside. If using canned beans, reserve for later use.

To roast the garlic, preheat an oven to 350° F. Slice the heads horizontally, cutting away the top one-fourth to expose individual cloves. Peel away the outer papery skin, leaving the garlic heads intact. Place in a small baking dish, rub generously with olive oil, and sprinkle with salt. Cover tightly with a lid or aluminum foil and bake for 45 minutes, then uncover and roast until soft, about 15 minutes longer. Remove from the oven and set aside. When cool enough to handle, squeeze the garlic from the skin into a small bowl.

Drain the beans and transfer 2 cups to a food processor or blender. (Cover and refrigerate or freeze any remaining beans for another purpose.) Add the roasted garlic and blend until fairly smooth. Season to taste with olive oil, salt, and pepper. Transfer to a small crock, garnish with parsley, and serve at room temperature with sliced bread.

Each recipe makes about 2 cups, enough for 8 servings.

Middle Eastern Garbanzo Spread (Hummus) with Pita Bread

Puréed garbanzo beans blended with sesame seed paste (tahini) is a quickly prepared and highly nutritious appetizer. Traditionally used as a spread or dip with pieces of pita bread, the mixture also goes well with crusty French bread, toasted whole-grain bread, or vegetables. Hummus can be thinned down with lemon juice and olive oil to taste for a tangy salad dressing or combined with plain yogurt for a sandwich spread.

Tahini is available in Greek or Middle Eastern specialty stores and most gourmet or natural-foods markets, as well as many supermarkets.

If using dried beans, cook as directed on page 18 and set aside. If using canned beans, reserve for later use.

In a food processor or blender, combine the sesame seed paste, the 2 tablespoons olive oil, and garlic and blend well. Drain the beans, reserving the liquid, and transfer 2 cups along with 1/2 cup of the reserved liquid to the sesame seed mixture. (Cover and refrigerate or freeze any remaining beans for another purpose.) Add the lemon juice and blend to a creamy consistency, adding more of the reserved bean liquid if necessary. Season to taste with salt and more lemon juice if needed. Cover and set aside at room temperature for about 2 hours.

In a small saucepan, combine the remaining 1/4 cup olive oil and the paprika. Place over medium heat and stir frequently until the oil turns red, about 3 minutes. Strain the oil through a fine-mesh sieve into a small bowl. Set aside.

To serve, spread the hummus on a serving plate. Using the back of a spoon, form an indentation in the center and fill with the red-tinted olive oil. Sprinkle with pomegranate seeds (if using) and garnish with mint sprigs. Serve with pita bread.

Makes 8 servings.

1 cup dried garbanzo beans, or 2 cups canned garbanzo beans

1/2 cup toasted sesame seed paste (tahini)

2 tablespoons plus 1/4 cup extra-virgin olive oil

1 tablespoon minced or pressed garlic

1/4 cup freshly squeezed lemon juice, or more if needed

Salt

1 tablespoon paprika

Pomegranate seeds for garnish (optional)

Fresh mint sprigs for garnish

Pita bread, preferably whole wheat, cut into small wedges

Bean-Filled Corn Shells *(Sopes)*

Masa is the dough made from hulled and softened dried corn kernels *(nixtamal)* that is used for making tortillas and tamales. Ready to use *masa* can often be purchased from a tortilla factory *(tortilleria)* or Mexican market, or see the recipe for making *nixtamal* for *masa* in *James McNair's Corn Cookbook.* Corn flour *(masa harina)*, made of dehydrated *masa*, is available in many supermarkets and makes a fine substitute.

Throughout Mexico, these crispy *masa* shells are known as *sopes*, as well as by a variety of other names depending upon their shape and origin. Elongated boat shapes are called *chalupas*. The same dough is also used to fashion round *gordas* or *gorditas*, or football-shaped *memelos*, small, fat tortillas over which the filling is spooned.

Cook the beans as directed. Set aside.

To make the *sopes*, if using fresh *masa*, place it in a mixing bowl. If using corn flour, place in a bowl and stir in just enough of the warm water to form a dough that holds together, cover, and set aside for about 30 minutes.

To the fresh or reconstituted *masa*, add the all-purpose flour, baking powder, salt, and lard, butter, or shortening. Using your hands, knead the mixture until well blended and light. If the mixture is too dry, add a little warm water. The finished dough should feel soft but not sticky.

Moisten your hands with water and form the dough into 12 walnut-sized balls. Place the balls in a bowl and cover tightly with plastic wrap.

Place a flat Mexican griddle *(comal)*, other griddle, or heavy skillet over medium heat. Moisten your hands with water. Working with 1 dough ball at a time, pat it between the palms of your hands into a flat disk about 3 inches in diameter and 1/4 inch thick, place it on the hot griddle, and cook until the bottom is partially set and lightly browned, about 1 minute. Turn and cook the other side until partially set, about 30 seconds. Remove to a work surface, last cooked side up, and pinch up the edge with your fingertips to form a 1/4 to 1/2 inch lip all around; dip your fingers in cold water if the dough is too hot to handle. Set aside. Cook and shape the remaining dough in the same way. At this time the *sopes* can be cooled, tightly covered, and refrigerated for up to 2 days.

1 1/2 cups Mexicali Beans (page 22) or Southwestern-Style Beans (page 23), each preferably made with black beans

SOPES

1 pound fresh *masa*, or 2 cups Mexican corn flour *(masa harina)*

About 1 1/3 cups warm water, if using corn flour

1/4 cup all-purpose flour, preferably unbleached

1 teaspoon baking powder

1/2 teaspoon salt

2 tablespoons lard, unsalted butter, or vegetable shortening

Canola oil or other high-quality vegetable oil for frying

CHERRY TOMATO SALSA

1 cup ripe cherry tomatoes, preferably a mixture of several colors and varieties

1/4 cup chopped green onion, including green tops

2 tablespoons chopped fresh serrano or other hot chile

2 tablespoons chopped fresh cilantro (coriander)

Salt

3/4 cup crumbled fresh Mexican cheese *(queso fresco)* or farmer cheese (about 3 ounces)

Fresh cilantro (coriander) sprigs for garnish

→

About 30 minutes before serving, prepare the salsa, begin to reheat the beans, and fry the *sopes.*

To make the salsa, slice the cherry tomatoes into halves or quarters, depending upon size. In a bowl, combine the tomatoes, green onion, chile, chopped cilantro, and salt to taste. Set aside. Drain just before using.

To fry the *sopes,* in a heavy skillet, pour in oil to a depth of about 1/2 inch and heat to 375° F, or until a small piece of bread dropped into the hot oil turns golden brown within about 30 seconds. Preheat an oven to 200° F. Position a wire rack over a baking sheet and place in the oven.

Carefully add a few of the *sopes* at a time to the hot oil; avoid crowding the pan. Fry until golden brown, 30 seconds to 1 minute. Using a slotted utensil, transfer to the wire rack in the oven to drain well and keep warm. Cook the remaining *sopes* in the same manner, allowing the oil to return to 375° F between batches.

Just before serving, drain the reheated beans and spoon about 2 tablespoons into each hot *sope* shell, then sprinkle with about 1 tablespoon cheese, and top with about 1 tablespoon of the drained salsa. Place on a serving dish or arrange on individual plates and garnish with cilantro sprigs.

Makes 6 servings.

Bagged Sushi *(Inari-zushi* or *Age-zushi)*

Auntie Naila Gallagher, who shared her Hawaiian version of this traditional Japanese sushi, calls this tasty snack "cone sushi," since the soybean bags serve as cones for the sweet-and-sour rice filling.

Light and airy fried soybean cakes, sometimes sold as tofu puffs, are not the same as pieces of dense, heavy fried soybean curd. Rice for sushi is cooked in less water than is called for in the basic recipe to allow for absorption of the vinegar mixture. If desired, add about 1 cup finely chopped cooked chicken or shrimp to the rice along with the vegetables.

To prepare the Soybean Cake Bags, cut each large rectangular cake in half crosswise, or make a slit along one side of each small square cake. Gently pull open the center of each to form a little bag. Transfer to a saucepan, add water to cover, place over medium-high heat, and bring to a boil. Reduce the heat to maintain a simmer and cook for about 15 minutes. Drain.

In a saucepan, combine the stock, broth, or water with the soy sauce, sugar, and salt (if using unsalted stock or water). Bring to a boil over medium-high heat. Add the soybean cake bags, adjust the heat to maintain a simmer, and cook, uncovered, carefully turning the bags occasionally, until they are soft and the liquid is absorbed, about 1 hour. Remove from the heat and let stand until cool. (At this point, the bags can be covered and refrigerated for up to 24 hours.)

To make the Sushi Rice, wash the rice as directed on page 31, then cover with cold water and soak for about 1 hour. Drain and cook the rice in 3 cups cold water as directed on page 31.

Just before the rice is ready, in a small saucepan, combine the vinegar, sugar, and salt. Place over medium-high heat and cook, stirring constantly, just until the sugar is dissolved, about 2 minutes; do not boil. Let cool briefly.

Fluff the warm rice with the tines of a fork and transfer it to a large mixing bowl. Pouring in a little at a time, add the vinegar mixture to the rice, turning the rice carefully with a wooden rice paddle or spatula to avoid crushing the kernels and to distribute the vinegar mixture evenly. Turn the rice continuously with the

$\longrightarrow$

SOYBEAN CAKE BAGS
12 large rectangular or 24 small square packaged fried soybean cakes *(aburage)*
1½ cups chicken or vegetable stock, canned reduced-sodium broth, or water
1 tablespoon soy sauce
3 tablespoons sugar
½ teaspoon salt (optional)

SUSHI RICE
3 cups medium-grain white rice
¾ cup unseasoned rice vinegar
¾ cup sugar
1 tablespoon salt

SEASONED VEGETABLES
3 tablespoons sugar
1½ teaspoons salt
¾ cup finely chopped or diced carrot
¾ cup thinly sliced green beans (cut crosswise)
1½ cups finely chopped fresh shiitake mushroom caps, or ¾ ounce dried Asian mushroom caps, rinsed thoroughly and soaked in warm water until soft, then finely chopped

Pickled ginger slices

paddle or spatula while fanning it with a paper or straw fan or a hair dryer set on cool until the rice is cool, about 5 minutes. Cover with a damp cloth towel and set aside at room temperature to absorb the vinegar mixture, at least 30 minutes or for up to several hours; do not refrigerate.

To make the Seasoned Vegetables, in a saucepan, combine the sugar, salt, and 3/4 cup water and bring to a boil over medium-high heat, stirring to dissolve the sugar and salt. Separately add and cook the carrot, green beans, and mushrooms, cooking each vegetable until tender but not mushy, about 5 minutes for the carrot and beans and about 2 minutes for the mushrooms. As soon as each vegetable is done, remove it with a wire skimmer, or drain it through a sieve, catching the liquid in a bowl and returning it to the saucepan and reheating for the next vegetable. Squeeze the mushrooms to remove excess liquid that can stain the rice. Gently combine the vegetables with the cooled rice.

Using your hands, squeeze each piece of soybean cake to release excess liquid; work carefully to prevent tearing bags. Moisten your hands with water and stuff about 1/3 cup of the rice mixture into each bag. Arrange the sushi on a tray, open side up. Garnish with pickled ginger or offer it alongside. Serve at room temperature.

Makes 8 servings.

Squash Blossoms Stuffed with Fava Beans and Bulgur

1 cup bulgur
1 cup shelled fresh or thawed frozen fava
    beans
2 tablespoons olive oil
1 cup chopped yellow onion
1 tablespoon minced or pressed garlic
1/2 cup golden raisins, soaked in hot water
    until plumped, then drained
1/2 cup pine nuts
1/2 cup chopped fresh mint
1/4 cup chopped fresh dill
2 tablespoons minced or grated fresh lemon
    zest
Salt
Freshly ground black pepper
Olive oil for brushing
About 24 squash blossoms
Fresh dill and/or mint sprigs for garnish
Blanched and peeled fresh fava beans for
    garnish (optional)
Plain yogurt

Inspired by several traditional Greek recipes, this summer treat is delicious hot or at room temperature. The stuffing is also delicious cold as a salad or heated as a side dish.

Green peas or lentils make appropriate substitutes for the fava beans, and 2 cups cooked white rice may be used in place of the bulgur. If you don't grow squash, look for blossoms in farmers' markets or specialty produce shops.

Prepare the bulgur as directed on page 34 and set aside.

Cook the beans as directed on page 11. Drain the cooked beans, mash with a fork to a coarse purée, and set aside.

In a sauté pan or heavy skillet, heat the 2 tablespoons olive oil over medium heat. Add the onion and sauté until soft, about 5 minutes. Add the garlic, raisins, and pine nuts and sauté for about 1 minute longer. Remove from the heat and stir in the mashed beans, bulgur, mint, dill, lemon zest, and salt and pepper to taste.

Preheat an oven to 375° F. Select a baking dish large enough to hold all of the squash blossoms later, brush with olive oil, and set aside.

Quickly rinse the squash blossoms under cold running water and gently pat dry with paper toweling. Using a small spoon, fill each squash blossom with the bean mixture, folding the ends of the petals over to enclose the stuffing. Arrange in a single layer in the prepared dish. Brush the squash blossoms with olive oil and drizzle with about 1/4 cup water. Cover tightly with a lid or aluminum foil and bake until the squash blossoms are tender, the stuffing is heated through, and most of the liquid has been absorbed, about 20 minutes.

Serve warm or at room temperature. Just before serving, garnish with herb sprigs and sprinkle with fava beans (if using). Offer yogurt at the table for spooning over the blossoms.

Makes 8 servings.

BOY GIRL

Black and White Salad

This satisfying combination is based on a medieval Spanish hot dish, *Moros y Cristianos*—Moors and Christians—in which black beans (the Moors) are served with white rice (the Christians).

For the photograph, the beans and rice were tossed separately, using half of the dressing and onion for each.

If using dried beans, cook as directed on page 18 and set aside to cool. If using canned beans, reserve for later use.

Cook the rice as directed on page 31 and set aside to cool.

To make the dressing, in a small bowl, combine all of the dressing ingredients and whisk to blend well. Set aside.

Drain the beans and transfer 3 cups to a large bowl. (Cover and refrigerate or freeze any remaining beans for another purpose.) Add the rice, onion, and the reserved dressing and toss to blend well. Cover and set aside at room temperature for about 1 hour, or refrigerate for up to 2 days; return to room temperature before serving.

To serve, mound the salad on a serving platter, garnish with red pepper (if using), and surround with cilantro sprigs.

Makes 6 servings.

1$\frac{1}{2}$ cups dried black beans, or 3 cups canned black beans
1 cup long-grain white rice

CUMIN DRESSING
$\frac{3}{4}$ cup extra-virgin olive oil
6 tablespoons freshly squeezed lemon juice
2$\frac{1}{4}$ teaspoons ground cumin
1$\frac{1}{2}$ teaspoons minced or pressed garlic
1$\frac{1}{2}$ teaspoons salt, or to taste
$\frac{1}{4}$ teaspoon freshly ground black pepper, or to taste
Bottled Louisiana-style hot sauce to taste

$\frac{3}{4}$ cup minced white onion
Red sweet pepper cutouts or strips for garnish (optional)
Fresh cilantro (coriander) sprigs for garnish

Taco Salad

4 cups Mexicali Beans (page 22)

TOMATO DRESSING
2/3 cup extra-virgin olive oil
1/3 cup red wine vinegar
3 tablespoons tomato paste
4 teaspoons sugar
1 teaspoon salt, or to taste
Freshly ground black pepper to taste

Romaine lettuce, separated into individual
    leaves, washed, dried, wrapped, and
    chilled to crisp, then torn into bite-sized
    pieces to equal 6 cups
2 cups peeled, seeded, drained and chopped
    firm, ripe tomato
1/2 cup chopped red onion
1/4 cup chopped fresh jalapeño or other hot
    chile
1/2 cup packed fresh cilantro (coriander)
    leaves
2 cups freshly shredded white Cheddar or
    Jack cheese (about 6 ounces)
6 cups lightly crushed white or yellow corn
    tortilla chips (about 8 ounces)

This Mexicali classic has been lightened for today's preferred dining style, but you may wish to add any favorite taco ingredient, such as seasoned, cooked ground beef or shredded chicken, sliced or chopped black olives, and dollops of sour cream or plain yogurt and/or guacamole.

See the variation for a southwestern twist to this refreshing main dish.

Cook the beans as directed and set aside to cool.

To make the dressing, in a small bowl, combine all of the dressing ingredients and whisk to blend well. Set aside.

Shortly before serving, in a large bowl, combine the lettuce, tomato, onion, chile, cilantro leaves, cheese, and tortilla chips and toss thoroughly. Drain the beans, add to the salad, and toss thoroughly. Add about half of the reserved dressing and toss to blend well. Pour the remaining dressing into a small pitcher.

To serve, transfer the salad to a large serving bowl and offer the extra dressing for drizzling over individual servings.

Makes 6 servings.

SOUTHWESTERN VARIATION: Use Southwestern-Style Beans (page 23) and blue corn tortilla chips. Substitute about 1 cup crumbled fresh goat cheese for the Cheddar or Jack cheese.

Couscous and Garbanzo Salad

Although Moroccan cooks would never turn their beloved couscous into a salad, the result of this preparation captures the essence of North African flavors. This recipe is based on a delectable main-course salad served by Dedie Carroll at Filoli, a spectacular National Trust mansion and garden.

For a heartier, nonvegetarian salad, poach 6 boned and skinned chicken breast halves in barely simmering chicken stock or canned reduced-sodium broth until just opaque throughout, about 12 minutes. Cool and shred the chicken, then stir it into the salad.

If using dried beans, cook as directed on page 18 and set aside to cool. If using canned beans, reserve for later use.

Prepare the couscous as directed on page 34 and set aside to cool.

To make the dressing, in a small bowl, combine all of the dressing ingredients and whisk to blend well. Set aside.

Drain the beans and transfer 3 cups to a large bowl. (Cover and refrigerate or freeze any remaining beans for another purpose.) Add the couscous, currants, sweet pepper, onion, mint, and parsley and mix well. Add the dressing and toss to distribute. Cover and let stand at room temperature for about 1 hour, or cover tightly and refrigerate for as long as overnight; return to room temperature before serving.

Place the pine nuts in a small, heavy skillet over medium heat. Toast, shaking the pan or stirring frequently, until lightly golden and fragrant, about 5 minutes. Pour onto a plate to cool.

Mound the salad on a serving dish or individual plates, sprinkle with the pine nuts, and garnish with tomato pieces.

Makes 6 main-dish servings, or 12 starter or side-dish servings.

1½ cups dried garbanzo beans, or 3 cups canned garbanzo beans
2 cups quick-cooking couscous

DRESSING
½ cup extra-virgin olive oil
½ cup freshly squeezed lemon juice
1 teaspoon minced or pressed garlic
½ teaspoon ground cumin
Bottled hot sauce, preferably North African *harissa*, to taste
Salt to taste
Freshly ground black pepper to taste

⅔ cup dried currants, soaked in hot water until plumped, then drained
⅔ cup finely chopped red sweet pepper
½ cup sliced green onion, including green tops
½ cup chopped fresh mint
½ cup chopped fresh flat-leaf parsley
½ cup pine nuts
Ripe tomato slices cut into small wedge-shaped pieces for garnish

Tomatoes Stuffed with Millet and Lentils

When garden-ripe tomatoes are at their peak, stuff them with this mixture brimming with Mediterranean flavors. When flavorful tomatoes are not available, the same combination can be used to fill sweet peppers or prebaked eggplants, or it makes a great salad or side dish on its own. Bulgur or couscous may be used instead of the millet.

Cook the lentils as directed on page 18 and set aside.

Cook the millet as directed on page 31 and set aside.

Slice the tops off the tomatoes. Using a spoon, carefully scoop out as much pulp as possible from the inside of each tomato, leaving a thin wall of pulp; avoid damaging the skin. Chop the pulp, then transfer to a colander or sieve to drain well. Set the tomatoes and their tops aside.

Drain the lentils and transfer 2 cups to a large bowl. (Cover and refrigerate or freeze any remaining lentils for another purpose.) Add the millet, drained tomato pulp, cheese, olives, garlic, olive oil, and lemon juice and toss to blend. Season to taste with salt and pepper. Just before serving, toss the chopped basil into the salad.

To serve cold, spoon the mixture into the tomato shells, place the tomato tops askew, and garnish with basil sprigs.

To serve warm, preheat an oven to 375° F. Stuff the tomatoes as above, place in a baking dish, drizzle with olive oil, and bake until the tomatoes are tender yet still hold their shape, about 20 minutes. Garnish with basil sprigs and serve immediately.

Makes 8 servings.

1 cup dried lentils, preferably French green type
½ cup millet
8 large ripe tomatoes, about 8 ounces each
½ cup crumbled feta cheese or fresh goat cheese
2 tablespoons chopped pitted Mediterranean-style olives, such as Kalamata or green Sicilian
1½ teaspoons minced or pressed garlic
¼ cup extra-virgin olive oil
2 tablespoons freshly squeezed lemon juice
Salt
Freshly ground black pepper
½ cup chopped fresh basil
Fresh basil sprigs for garnish

Succotash Chowder

2 tablespoons unsalted butter

2 cups chopped leek, including pale green portion, or yellow onion

4 cups fresh corn kernels, cut from about 6 medium-sized ears, cobs reserved

3 cups shelled fresh or thawed frozen baby lima beans or butter beans

3 cups milk

3 cups vegetable or chicken stock, canned reduced-sodium broth, or water

4 or 5 fresh summer savory or thyme sprigs

4 fresh flat-leaf parsley sprigs

4 ounces sliced bacon or baked ham (optional)

1½ cups peeled, seeded, drained, and chopped ripe or canned tomato

Salt

Freshly ground black pepper

Minced fresh chives for garnish

Slivered leek, including pale green portion, fried in high-quality vegetable oil until golden and crisp, for garnish (optional)

Native Americans lent the name succotash to the early colonial side dish that teams lima beans with corn. Here those ingredients are turned into a thick and flavorful soup.

In a large pot, melt the butter over medium-high heat. Add the leek or onion and sauté until soft, about 5 minutes. Add the corn kernels and lima or butter beans and sauté about 2 minutes. Add the reserved corn cobs, milk, and stock, broth, or water. Tie the herb sprigs together and add to the pot. Bring almost to a boil, then adjust the heat to maintain a simmer and cook, uncovered, until the corn and beans are very tender, about 35 minutes.

If using bacon, cut crosswise into pieces about ½ inch wide. Transfer to a sauté pan or heavy skillet and cook over medium heat, stirring frequently, until crisp, 6 to 7 minutes. Using a slotted utensil, transfer the bacon to paper toweling to drain. If using ham, cut into thin slivers and set aside.

Remove and discard the corn cobs and herb sprigs from the soup. Working in batches, transfer the soup to a food processor or blender and blend as smoothly as possible. For a smoother soup, put the blended mixture through a food mill, sieve, or conical *chinois*. Transfer to a clean saucepan, add the tomato, season to taste with salt and pepper, and simmer over medium heat until heated through, about 8 minutes.

To serve, ladle the soup into warmed bowls and sprinkle with the reserved bacon or slivered ham (if using), chives, and/or fried leek (if using).

Makes 6 servings.

Creamy Red Bean Soup
with Crispy Rice Croutons

Use this idea with any of the Well-Seasoned Beans (pages 21-23) and other cooked grains.

Cook the beans until very tender as directed, using enough stock or water to cover the beans by about 3 inches. Meanwhile, cook the rice as directed on page 31 and set aside to cool slightly; do not refrigerate.

When the beans are ready, discard the ham and sausage or reserve for another purpose. Working in batches if necessary, transfer the beans and 4 cups of their liquid to a food processor or blender and blend as smoothly as possible. Position a food mill, sieve, or conical *chinois* over a saucepan, add the bean purée, and grind or press to release as much liquid as possible. Stir in additional bean liquid if necessary to achieve a creamy consistency. Place over low heat.

In a sauté pan or skillet, pour in oil to a depth of ¹/₂ inch. Heat to 375° F, or until a small piece of bread dropped into the hot oil turns golden within 30 seconds. While the oil is heating, crack the egg into a mixing bowl and beat lightly. Add the cooled rice and salt and pepper to taste and mix thoroughly. Moisten your hands with water. Using about ¹/₄ cup of the rice mixture, form a round patty about 3 inches in diameter between the palms of your hands and place it on a metal spatula. Using another spatula or slotted utensil, carefully slide the rice crouton into the hot oil. Repeat this procedure to add 2 or 3 more croutons; avoid crowding the pan. Cook until the bottoms of the croutons are crisp and golden brown, about 1 minute, then carefully turn and cook until the other sides are crisp and golden brown, about 1 minute longer. Using a slotted utensil, remove the croutons to a wire rack to drain well. Cook the remaining rice in the same manner, allowing the oil to return to 375° F between batches, to make a total of 8 croutons.

To serve, ladle the soup into 4 warmed bowls, add 2 rice croutons to each serving, sprinkle with minced chives or green onion, and garnish with whole chives (if using).

Makes 4 servings.

New Orleans-Style Beans (page 22)
1 cup long-grain white rice
Canola oil or other high-quality vegetable oil for frying
1 egg
Salt
Freshly ground black pepper
Minced fresh chives or green onion, including green tops, for garnish
Whole fresh chives for garnish (optional)

Provençal Bean and Pasta Soup
(Soupe au Pistou)

2 cups dried small white beans, preferably
  *flageolet*s

2 cups finely chopped leek, including pale
  green portion

1 tablespoon chopped garlic

4 fresh flat-leaf parsley sprigs

4 fresh basil sprigs

About 2 quarts (8 cups) unsalted chicken or
  vegetable stock for cooking beans
  (optional)

1½ cups diced boiling potato

1½ cups diced zucchini or other summer
  squash

1½ cups diced carrot

6 ounces fresh green beans, trimmed and cut
  into ½-inch lengths

Salt

Freshly ground black pepper

About 1 quart (4 cups) chicken or vegetable
  stock or canned reduced-sodium broth
  for finishing soup

3 ounces dried tiny pasta *(pastina)* or small
  macaroni

BASIL PASTE *(PISTOU)*

2 cups packed fresh basil leaves

4 teaspoons chopped garlic

¾ cup freshly grated Parmesan cheese,
  preferably Parmigiano-Reggiano (about
  3 ounces)

6 tablespoons extra-virgin olive oil

Salt

Freshly ground black pepper

The French name for this simple, earthy potage comes from the Provençal basil paste, or *pistou*, that is stirred into the finished soup. *Pistou* is similar to the more famous Italian *pesto*, except that pine nuts are omitted from the French version and tomatoes are often added. If you wish to add tomatoes, peel, seed, drain, and chop 8 ounces ripe tomatoes and blend along with the basil. When dicing the vegetables, cut them about the same size as the beans.

Clean and soak the beans as described on page 18. Drain and transfer to a large, heavy saucepan or soup pot. Add the leek, garlic, parsley and basil sprigs, and enough unsalted stock or water to cover by about ½ inch. Place over medium-high heat and bring to a boil, then reduce the heat to maintain a simmer, cover partially, and cook, stirring occasionally, until the beans are tender, about 1 hour.

Stir the potato, squash, carrot, and green beans into the beans. Season to taste with salt and pepper and add enough of the stock or broth to cover by about 2 inches. Bring to a boil over medium-high heat, then reduce the heat to maintain a simmer, cover, and cook, stirring occasionally, until the vegetables are tender, about 20 minutes longer. Add additional stock, broth, or water at any time during cooking if necessary to maintain a soupy consistency.

Stir the pasta into the simmering soup and cook until the pasta is tender yet firm to the bite, 5 to 10 minutes, depending upon type and size of pasta.

Meanwhile, make the *pistou*. In a food processor or blender, combine the basil, garlic, cheese, and olive oil and blend as smoothly as possible. Season to taste with salt and pepper. Transfer to a small bowl.

Discard the herb sprigs from the soup, ladle it into preheated bowls, and serve piping hot. Offer the *pistou* at the table for diners to add to taste. Alternatively, stir the *pistou* to taste into the simmering soup just before serving.

Makes 8 servings.

Indian Lentils *(Dal)* with Rice

Very good

2 cups red lentils *(masoor dal)*

2 tablespoons clarified butter *(ghee)* or high-quality vegetable oil

2 cups finely chopped shallot or red onion

1/4 cup finely chopped fresh ginger

1 tablespoon minced fresh serrano or other hot chile, or to taste

2 teaspoons minced or pressed garlic

2 teaspoons ground coriander

1 teaspoon ground turmeric

1 teaspoon ground cumin

1 teaspoon ground cayenne pepper, or to taste

1 teaspoon freshly ground black pepper, or to taste

1/2 teaspoon ground cardamom

1/2 teaspoon ground cinnamon

1/4 teaspoon ground cloves

1/4 teaspoon freshly grated nutmeg

2 quarts (8 cups) hot water

2 cups peeled, seeded, drained, and chopped ripe or canned tomato

Salt

3 cups long-grain white rice, preferably *basmati*

Canola oil or other high-quality vegetable oil for frying (if cooking *papadams)*

About 16 *papadams* (optional)

2 tablespoons freshly squeezed lime juice, or to taste

1/2 cup chopped fresh cilantro (coriander)

Fresh cilantro leaves for garnish

Although lentils *(dal)* combined with rice could be described as the national dish of India, the preparation varies from house to house. In some versions the lentils are puréed after cooking, but in this style they remain whole. For a drier result, add only enough liquid to cover the lentils by 1/2 inch. Alternative traditional legumes include split mung beans *(moong dal)*, yellow split peas *(chana dal)*, black-eyed peas, small red beans, and garbanzo beans.

Crisp wafers made from ground dried lentils or a combination of lentils and rice flour *(papadams)*, available from Indian markets or some gourmet stores, are a traditional accompaniment.

Pick over, rinse, and drain the lentils as described on page 18 and set aside.

In a heavy-bottomed saucepan, heat 2 tablespoons of the clarified butter or oil over medium-high heat. Add the shallot or onion, ginger, and chile and sauté until very soft and golden, about 8 minutes. Add the garlic, ground spices, and nutmeg and sauté about 1 minute longer. Add the lentils and hot water and bring to a boil. Adjust the heat to maintain a simmer, cover, and cook, stirring occasionally, until the lentils are just tender, about 10 minutes. Add the tomato and salt to taste and continue to cook, uncovered, until the lentils are very soft, about 10 minutes longer.

Meanwhile, cook the rice as directed on page 31.

To cook the *papadams* (if using), in a wok, deep-fat fryer, or sauté pan, pour in oil to a depth of 1 inch. Heat to 365° F, or until a small piece of bread dropped into the hot oil turns golden within 30 seconds. Carefully add a *papadam* to the hot oil and cook just until puffed, about 3 seconds; do not allow to brown. Using tongs, transfer the *papadam* to a wire rack to drain well. Cook the remaining *papadams* in the same manner, allowing the oil to return to 375° F between each.

Remove the lentils from the heat. Stir in the lime juice, chopped cilantro, and more salt if needed. Ladle into individual bowls or deep plates, add a scoop of the hot rice to each serving, and garnish with cilantro leaves. Serve the *papadams* (if used) alongside.

Makes 8 servings.

Bean and Barley "Risotto"

Cooking pearled barley in the manner of an Italian risotto turns the grain creamy, similar to Arborio rice.

If using fresh beans or peas, cook as directed on page 11, then plunge into iced water to halt cooking and set aside. If using dried beans, cook as directed on page 18 and set aside. If using canned beans, reserve for later use.

Wash and drain the barley as directed on page 31.

In a saucepan, bring the stock or broth to a boil over high heat, then reduce the heat to low and keep the broth at a simmer while cooking the barley.

In a heavy sauté pan or deep skillet, melt the butter over medium-high heat. Add the onion and mushrooms and sauté until the onion is soft and the mushrooms are tender, about 5 minutes. Add the garlic and barley and sauté until all the grains of the barley are well coated, about 2 minutes. Stir in the wine and cook, stirring, until the wine has evaporated, about 3 minutes. Add 1/2 cup of the simmering stock or broth, adjusting the heat under the barley if the liquid is evaporating too quickly. Keep the barley at a simmer and stir almost continuously, scraping the bottom and sides of the pan, until the liquid has been absorbed.

Continue to add the stock or broth 1/2 cup at a time each time the barley becomes dry, and continue to stir the barley as it cooks. As the "risotto" approaches completion, add the stock or broth only 1/4 cup at a time. You may not need it all before the barley is done, or you may need more, in which case add hot water. Cook until the barley is tender but firm to the bite, about 30 minutes in all. About 5 minutes before the barley is done, drain the beans or peas and stir them into the simmering barley. When the barley is done, add the cheese and stir for about 2 minutes. The completed dish should be creamy but not soupy; if it is too dry, add a little more stock or broth or hot water. Season with salt and pepper to taste. Shower with parsley and serve immediately. Pass additional Parmesan cheese at the table.

Makes 4 servings.

2 cups sliced fresh green beans (1/2-inch lengths), shelled fresh or thawed frozen green (English) peas, or shelled fresh fava beans or other fresh beans; 1 cup dried white beans such as *cannellini*; or 2 cups canned small white beans

Iced water (if using fresh beans or peas)

1 cup pearled barley

6 to 8 cups meat, chicken, or vegetable stock or canned reduced-sodium broth

3 tablespoons unsalted butter

1/2 cup chopped shallot or yellow onion

1 1/2 cups chopped fresh mushrooms, preferably porcini, portobello, or similar flavorful variety

1 teaspoon minced or pressed garlic

1/2 cup dry white wine

2/3 cup freshly grated Parmesan cheese, preferably Parmigiano-Reggiano (about 3 ounces)

Salt

Freshly ground black pepper

Minced fresh flat-leaf parsley for garnish

Freshly grated Parmesan cheese, preferably Parmigiano-Reggiano, for serving

Chinese Green Beans and Pork in Garlic-Chile Sauce with Rice

2 cups long-grain white rice

1 pound fresh tender Asian long beans or other green beans

1/2 cup soy sauce

3 tablespoons sugar

2 tablespoons unseasoned rice vinegar

2 tablespoons cornstarch

2 tablespoons canola oil or other high-quality vegetable oil

8 ounces minced or ground lean pork

1/4 cup chopped garlic

2 teaspoons crushed dried hot chile or Asian chile paste or sauce, or to taste

1/2 cup sliced green onion, including green tops

To turn this fiery dish into vegetarian fare, omit the pork.

Cook the rice as directed on page 31.

Meanwhile, cut off and discard both ends from each bean. If necessary, pull off any strings. Cut the beans crosswise into 1-inch lengths and set aside.

In a small bowl, stir together the soy sauce, sugar, vinegar, cornstarch, and 1/2 cup water; set aside.

Place a wok, large sauté pan, or large, heavy skillet over high heat. When the pan is hot, add 1 tablespoon of the oil and swirl to coat the pan. When the oil is hot but not yet smoking, add the pork and stir-fry until the meat turns opaque, 2 to 3 minutes. Remove to a bowl and set aside.

Add the remaining 1 tablespoon oil to the pan. When it is hot but not yet smoking, add the green beans and stir-fry until well coated with oil, about 1 minute. Add the garlic, dried chile or chile paste or sauce, and 2 tablespoons water, cover, and cook, stirring occasionally, until the beans are crisp-tender, 2 to 3 minutes, depending on type and size of beans. Uncover and stir in the cooked pork. Stir the reserved soy sauce mixture to recombine, then stir it into the beans. Add the green onion and cook, stirring frequently, until the sauce comes to a boil. Then continue cooking, stirring constantly, until the sauce thickens, 1 to 2 minutes. Transfer to a serving bowl and serve with the rice.

Makes 4 servings.

Hoppin' John

The origin of the odd name of this southern classic, often served as a traditional New Year's good luck dish, has long been gone with the wind.

1½ cups dried black-eyed peas, or
    3 cups shelled fresh or thawed frozen
    black-eyed peas
4 ounces sliced bacon or slab bacon,
    trimmed of rind
1½ cups chopped yellow onion
1 cup chopped celery
1 cup chopped red or green sweet pepper
1 tablespoon minced or pressed garlic
1 tablespoon minced fresh thyme, or
    1 teaspoon crumbled dried thyme
1 bay leaf
1 cup long-grain white rice
1½ cups chicken or vegetable stock or
    canned reduced-sodium broth
2 cups peeled, seeded, drained, and chopped
    ripe or canned tomato
Salt
Freshly ground black pepper
Bottled Louisiana-style hot sauce
¾ cup chopped green onion, including
    green tops
½ cup chopped fresh flat-leaf parsley
Fresh flat-leaf parsley sprigs for garnish

If using dried peas, clean and soak as directed on page 18, drain, and set aside. If using fresh or frozen peas, reserve for later use.

If using sliced bacon, cut crosswise into pieces about ½ inch wide. If using slab bacon, cut into ¼-inch dice. Transfer to a heavy saucepan and cook over medium heat, stirring frequently, until browned and crisp, 6 to 7 minutes. Using a slotted utensil, transfer the bacon to paper toweling to drain.

Discard all but 3 tablespoons of the bacon fat (or save for another use) and place the saucepan over medium-high heat. Add the onion, celery, and sweet pepper and sauté until the vegetables are soft, about 5 minutes. Stir in the peas, garlic, thyme, bay leaf, and just enough water to cover barely. Bring to a boil, then reduce the heat to maintain a simmer and cook, partially covered, until the peas are tender but still hold their shape, 15 to 25 minutes.

Meanwhile, cook the rice in the stock or broth as directed on page 31.

Stir the tomato into the peas and simmer, uncovered, about 5 minutes. Stir in the rice, season to taste with salt and generous amounts of ground pepper and hot sauce, and heat through, about 2 minutes. Stir in most of the green onion and chopped parsley. Transfer to a serving dish, sprinkle with the reserved bacon and the remaining green onion and chopped parsley, garnish with parsley sprigs, and serve immediately.

Makes 6 servings.

VEGETARIAN VARIATION: Omit the bacon. Substitute 3 tablespoons canola oil or other high-quality vegetable oil for the bacon renderings. Cook the rice in vegetable stock or water.

Spanish Rice with Green Beans and Peas

3 tablespoons olive oil

1 large yellow onion, sliced vertically into thin wedges

2 large red sweet peppers, stems, membranes, and seeds discarded, sliced lengthwise into 1/4-inch-wide strips

10 ounces chorizo or other spicy pork sausage, casings discarded, sliced about 1/2-inch thick

1/2 cup drained and chopped sun-dried tomatoes packed in olive oil

1 tablespoon minced or pressed garlic

2 cups short-grain white rice, preferably Spanish Valencia

3 cups chicken or vegetable stock or canned reduced-sodium broth

1 cup dry white wine

1/4 cup minced fresh flat-leaf parsley

1 tablespoon tomato paste

1 teaspoon paprika

1/2 teaspoon saffron threads (optional)

Salt

Freshly ground black pepper

1 pound fresh green beans, trimmed and cut crosswise into 3/4-inch lengths

Iced water

2 cups tender shelled fresh or thawed frozen green (English) peas

3/4 cup sliced, pitted brine-packed ripe olives

Chopped fresh flat-leaf parsley for garnish

Shredded fresh orange zest for garnish

This combination captures the zesty essence of Spanish Mediterranean cooking.

Preheat an oven to 375° F.

In a sauté pan or large, heavy skillet, heat the oil over medium-high heat. Add the onion and sweet peppers and sauté until soft, about 5 minutes. Add the chorizo, sun-dried tomatoes, and garlic and sauté about 2 minutes longer. Add the rice and sauté until the grains are well coated, about 5 minutes. Stir in the stock or broth, wine, parsley, tomato paste, paprika, saffron (if using), and salt and pepper to taste. Bring to a boil, stirring constantly, then transfer to a large, shallow baking dish, preferably made of earthenware. Cover tightly with a lid or aluminum foil and bake for 20 minutes.

Meanwhile, in a saucepan, bring about 4 cups water to a boil over medium-high heat. Add the green beans and cook until barely crisp-tender, 5 to 10 minutes, depending upon size and variety of beans. Drain and immerse in iced water to halt cooking, then drain well.

Remove the rice from the oven, uncover, and add the beans, peas, and olives, stirring well to distribute the ingredients evenly. Cover tightly, return to the oven, and bake until the liquid is absorbed and the rice is tender, about 10 minutes; if the rice gets too dry before it is done, add a bit more stock, broth, or water. Remove from the oven and let stand about 10 minutes.

Just before serving, sprinkle the warm rice with the chopped parsley and orange zest.

Makes 8 servings.

Chiles Stuffed with Beans and Corn
(Chiles Rellenos con Frijoles y Maiz)

Most of us who reside north of the Rio Grande are familiar with battered and fried *chiles rellenos*. Mexican cooks, however, usually omit the batter and frying when chiles are stuffed with ingredients other than cheese.

Cook the beans as directed and set aside.

To make the Roasted Tomato Salsa, preheat an oven to 350° F and line a baking sheet with aluminum foil or kitchen parchment. Place the tomatoes, cut side down, on the prepared baking sheet and roast until the tomatoes are very shriveled and fairly dry but not burned, 1 to 1½ hours. Remove from the oven and let cool briefly, then remove and discard the skins and transfer the pulp to a food processor or blender.

In a small saucepan, heat the oil over medium-high heat. Add the onion and chopped chile and sauté until the onion is golden and very soft, about 8 minutes. Add the garlic and sauté about 1 minute longer. Transfer to the food processor or blender with the roasted tomato pulp and blend until fairly smooth. Return the mixture to the pan, season to taste with salt and pepper, and set aside.

Place the chiles over a charcoal fire, directly over a gas flame, or under a preheated broiler. Roast, turning several times, until the skin is charred all over. Transfer the chiles to a paper bag, close the bag loosely, and let stand for about 10 minutes.

Drain the beans. In a bowl, combine the beans, corn, cheese, chopped cilantro, and salt and pepper to taste. Set aside.

Using your fingertips, rub away the charred skin from the chiles. Leaving the stems intact, carefully slit each chile lengthwise down one side. Using your fingertips, remove the seeds and veins, being careful not to tear the chile skin. Sprinkle the insides of the chiles with salt to taste.

Preheat an oven to 350° F. Select a baking dish large enough to hold all of the chiles and lightly brush with olive oil.

→

1½ cups Mexicali Beans (page 22) or Southwestern-Style Beans (page 23)

ROASTED TOMATO SALSA
4 pounds ripe tomatoes, cored, cut in half crosswise, seeded, and drained

4 teaspoons olive oil, preferably extra-virgin

1½ cups chopped white onion

¼ cup chopped fresh jalapeño or other hot chile, or to taste

2 teaspoons chopped garlic

Salt

Freshly ground black pepper

8 large, mild green or red chiles, preferably *poblano*

1½ cups fresh corn kernels (cut from about 2 cobs)

1 cup freshly shredded Jack or white Cheddar cheese (about 3 ounces)

¼ cup finely chopped fresh cilantro (coriander)

Salt

Freshly ground black pepper

Olive oil for brushing

Mexican cultured cream *(crema)* or crème fraîche, placed in a squeeze bottle

Fresh epazote, cilantro (coriander), or flat-leaf parsley sprigs for garnish

Stuff each chile with an equal portion of the bean-corn mixture. Transfer seam side down to the prepared baking dish and lightly brush with olive oil. Bake until the filling is heated through, about 20 minutes.

To serve, reheat the Roasted Tomato Salsa and spoon it onto warmed individual plates. Arrange the chiles on top of each portion, squeeze the cream or crème fraîche over the chiles to create an interesting pattern, and garnish with the herb sprigs. Serve immediately.

Makes 8 appetizer servings, or 4 main dish servings.

Cornbread-Crusted Bean Chili

This hearty chili may also be prepared from pinto beans or a combination of beans and topped with any favorite cornbread recipe. For smaller groups, the recipe can be cut in half and baked in an 8-inch square baking pan or 2-quart baking dish (although you may want to make the full recipe since leftovers reheat well). The chili also makes a satisfying dish without the cornbread topping; ladle into preheated bowls without draining after cooking.

To make the Bean Chili, if using dried beans, cook the beans as directed on page 18 and set aside. If using canned beans, reserve for later use.

In a small skillet, combine the cumin seed, oregano, ground chile, cayenne, and paprika. Place over medium heat and toast, stirring or shaking the pan frequently, until fragrant, about 5 minutes; do not allow to burn. Pour onto a plate to cool, then transfer to a spice grinder or heavy mortar with a pestle and grind to a fine powder. Set aside.

In a large, heavy pot, heat the oil over medium-high heat. Add the onion and sauté until soft, about 5 minutes. Add the garlic and reserved spice mixture and sauté about 1 minute longer. Stir in the tomato and *chipotle* chile and bring to a boil, then reduce the heat to achieve a simmer and cook, stirring occasionally, for about 15 minutes.

Transfer 6 cups of the cooked or canned beans and their liquid to the mixture. (Cover and refrigerate or freeze any remaining beans for another purpose.) Add water if needed to cover the beans barely. Simmer until the mixture is well flavored, about 30 minutes.

Preheat an oven to 350° F. Grease a 3-quart shallow baking dish, a 9-by-13-inch baking pan, or 8 individual-sized baking dishes.

Remove the chili from the heat and stir in the lime juice or vinegar and chopped cilantro. Taste and adjust seasonings. Drain in a colander or sieve to remove excess liquid, which can be saved for adding to a soup or other dish. Transfer the drained chili to the prepared baking dish(es). Set aside.

→

BEAN CHILI

3 cups dried black beans, or 6 cups canned black beans

1½ tablespoons cumin seed

1½ tablespoons dried oregano

3 tablespoons ground dried chile, such as *ancho* or *pasilla*, preferably freshly ground

½ teaspoon cayenne pepper

1½ tablespoons paprika

3 tablespoons olive oil

3 cups chopped yellow onion

2 teaspoons minced or pressed garlic

4 cups peeled, seeded, drained and chopped ripe or canned tomato

1 teaspoon chopped canned *chipotle* chile in *adobo* sauce

1 tablespoon freshly squeezed lime juice or red wine vinegar

¼ cup chopped fresh cilantro (coriander)

TEX-MEX CORNBREAD

1 cup yellow cornmeal, preferably stone-
  ground

1 cup all-purpose flour, preferably
  unbleached

2 tablespoons sugar

1 tablespoon baking powder

1 teaspoon salt

2 eggs

1/2 cup sour cream or plain yogurt

1/4 cup (1/2 stick) unsalted butter, melted, or
  canola oil or other high-quality vegetable
  oil

2 cups fresh, thawed frozen, or drained
  canned corn kernels

2 cups freshly shredded Cheddar cheese
  (about 6 ounces)

1/2 cup grated yellow onion

1/4 cup minced fresh or canned hot chile such
  as jalapeño or serrano

Fresh cilantro (coriander) sprigs or leaves for
  garnish

To make the Tex-Mex Cornbread, in a large mixing bowl, combine the cornmeal, flour, sugar, baking powder, and salt; mix well. Add the eggs, sour cream or yogurt, melted butter or oil, corn, cheese, onion, and chile and stir just until the mixture is blended; do not overmix.

Spread the cornbread batter evenly over the top of the chili, dividing it equally if using individual baking dishes. Bake until golden brown and a wooden skewer inserted into the center of the cornbread layer comes out clean, about 45 minutes. Garnish with cilantro sprigs or leaves and serve hot.

Makes 8 servings.

Bean and Berry Casserole

Whether you call this hearty combination of whole-grain berries and beans a casserole, *gratin*, or *tian* depends upon the style of baking dish you use.

Cook the rye, triticale, or wheat as directed on page 31.

If using dried beans, cook as directed on page 18 and set aside. If using canned beans, reserve for later use.

To make the white sauce, in a heavy-bottomed saucepan, melt the butter over low heat. Add the flour and whisk briskly to blend until smooth; do not brown. Add the milk all at once and whisk until very smooth. Season to taste with salt, pepper, and nutmeg (if using). Simmer, stirring frequently, until thickened to the consistency of heavy cream, about 10 minutes. Set aside.

In a heavy-bottomed sauté pan or heavy skillet, melt the 3 tablespoons butter over medium-high heat. Add the mushrooms, leek, and carrot and sauté for about 2 minutes. Reduce the heat to medium-low and cook until the mushrooms are tender, 5 to 10 minutes longer, depending upon the mushroom variety.

Preheat an oven to 375° F. Butter a porcelain-glazed *gratin*, glazed red *tian*, or other ovenproof casserole dish; choose an oval about 10 by 14 inches, a 9-by-13-inch rectangle, or a 3-quart round dish. Alternatively, prepare 8 individual-sized baking dishes.

Drain the cooked or canned beans and transfer 2 cups to a mixing bowl. (Cover and refrigerate or freeze any remaining beans for another purpose.) Add the cooked grain, mushroom mixture, white sauce, minced parsley, and minced or crumbled thyme and stir to blend well. Season to taste with salt and pepper. Transfer the mixture to the prepared dish(es) and sprinkle evenly with the cheese, or sprinkle with the bread crumbs and drizzle with olive oil. Bake until the top is bubbly and begins to brown, about 25 minutes. If using bread crumbs, the dish can be placed under a preheated broiler during the last few minutes to create a crispier crust.

Just before serving, garnish with herb sprigs.

Makes 8 servings.

1 cup rye, triticale, or wheat berries
1 cup dried small white beans such as *cannellini* or *flageolets*, or 2 cups canned small white beans

WHITE SAUCE
5 tablespoons unsalted butter
5 tablespoons all-purpose flour
3 cups milk
Salt
Freshly ground white or black pepper
Freshly grated nutmeg (optional)

3 tablespoons unsalted butter
8 ounces fresh wild mushrooms, such as chanterelle, porcini, or shiitake, finely chopped
1 cup finely chopped leek, including pale green portion
1 cup finely chopped carrot
1/2 cup minced fresh flat-leaf parsley
1 tablespoon minced fresh thyme, or 1 teaspoon crumbled dried thyme
Salt
Freshly ground white or black pepper
Softened butter for greasing
2 cups freshly shredded Gruyère or other good-melting cheese, or 2 cups fine fresh bread crumbs
Extra-virgin olive oil for drizzling, if using bread crumbs
Fresh thyme or flat-leaf parsley sprigs for garnish

Boston Baked Beans with Brown Bread

Boston Baked Beans (page 26)

BROWN BREAD
Unsalted butter for greasing
1/2 cup whole-wheat flour
1/2 cup medium rye flour
1 teaspoon baking soda
1/2 teaspoon salt
1/2 cup yellow or white cornmeal, preferably
    stone-ground
1 cup buttermilk
1/3 cup unsulphured light molasses
1 tablespoon unsalted butter, melted
1/2 cup raisins, soaked in dark rum or hot
    water until plumped, then drained
Fresh bay leaves or flat-leaf parsley sprigs for
    garnish

Here is a classic combination that draws upon recipes popular in colonial America.

Although home cooks have long relied on coffee cans as handy containers for cooking brown bread, recent reports indicate that cans may release harmful toxins when heated. Safe options include metal pudding molds, heatproof bowls, and tempered glass can-shaped containers available from baking-supply catalogs and some cookware stores. You may wish to use a 2-quart container and double the bread recipe and cooking time.

Cook the beans as directed.

About 2 hours before the beans are done, prepare for cooking the Brown Bread. Select a 1-quart pudding mold or other container (see recipe introduction) and a pot with a tight-fitting cover large enough to hold the container. Place a flat steaming rack in the bottom of the pot. Place the container on the rack and add enough water to reach about halfway up the sides of the container, then remove the container and set it aside. Place the pot over high heat and bring the water to a boil, then cover and adjust the heat to maintain a simmer.

To make the Brown Bread, generously butter the container and set aside. Sift together the flours, baking soda, and salt into a mixing bowl. Stir in the cornmeal. Add the buttermilk, molasses, butter, and raisins and stir to blend well. Spoon the mixture into the buttered container, filling no more than two-thirds full. If using a pudding mold with a lid, cover with the lid; if using a mold or other container without a lid, cover tightly with aluminum foil. Place the container on the rack inside the pot of simmering water. Cover and simmer until a wooden skewer inserted in the center of the bread comes out clean, about 1 1/2 hours; adjust the heat to maintain simmering water throughout cooking, adding boiling water if needed to maintain water level.

Transfer the container to a wire rack, remove the lid or foil, and let stand for about 5 minutes, then turn the bread out onto the rack to cool a few minutes longer. Using a serrated bread knife, slice the warm bread and serve with the beans. Garnish individual servings with bay leaves or parsley sprigs.

Makes 4 main-dish servings, or 8 side-dish servings.

Creamy Tofu Mousse with Granola Crunch

2 cups Sunshine Granola (page 35)

CREAMY TOFU MOUSSE
1 pound firm tofu (see recipe introduction), drained
3/4 cup sugar
2 teaspoons pure vanilla extract
8 ounces high-quality semisweet, bittersweet, or white chocolate, melted; 1/4 cup unsweetened cocoa powder, preferably Dutch-process type; or 2 tablespoons instant espresso powder

Fresh mint sprigs or leaves for garnish
Fresh orange zest for garnish

The texture of tofu (soybean curd) varies with the manufacturer; look for a silky, fine-textured product to create a satiny smooth dessert. For an attractive presentation, make two batches in contrasting flavors and alternately layer or swirl them together.

Prepare the Sunshine Granola as directed and set aside.

To make the mousse, place the tofu in a food processor or blender and blend until smooth and creamy. Add the sugar and vanilla and blend well.

For rich chocolate mousse, add the melted chocolate and blend well.

For low-fat chocolate mousse, add the cocoa powder and blend well.

For espresso mousse, add the espresso powder and blend well.

For mocha mousse, add either the melted chocolate or cocoa powder and the espresso powder and blend well.

Cover and refrigerate until well chilled, about 2 hours or up to 2 days.

To serve, alternately spoon the mousse and granola into tall clear glasses to create several layers, ending with a sprinkling of the granola. Garnish with mint sprigs or leaves and orange zest.

Makes 6 servings.

Gingerbeanbread with Ginger Crunch Topping

This very moist, dark cake, topped with a crisp, tantalizing crust, features a fusion of peppery amaranth and sweet *azuki* beans that yields a flavor-packed, protein-rich treat. For a less exotic version, substitute all-purpose or whole-wheat flour for the amaranth flour and use white or other mild-flavored beans.

If desired, serve with plain or vanilla-flavored yogurt, whipped cream, or your favorite gingerbread topping or sauce.

To make the Gingerbeanbread, cook the beans in water until very tender as directed on page 18; do not season. Drain, transfer to a food processor or blender, and purée as smoothly as possible. Transfer the purée to a food mill, sieve, or conical *chinois* set over a bowl and grind or press into the bowl to remove the skins. Set aside.

Preheat an oven to 350° F. Grease an 8-inch square baking pan.

In a bowl, combine the flours, baking powder, baking soda, and salt and mix well.

In the bowl of an electric mixer, combine the bean purée, molasses, sugar, butter or oil, egg, and ginger and mix well. Add the flour mixture and beat on medium speed just until the batter is smooth, about 1 minute; do not overbeat. Pour the batter into the prepared pan. Bake until the top of the cake is set, about 30 minutes.

Meanwhile, prepare the Ginger Crunch Topping. In a small bowl, combine the ginger and sugar and mix well.

Remove the cake from the oven and distribute the topping evenly over it. Return the cake to the oven and bake until a sharp knife inserted into the center comes out almost clean, about 30 minutes longer. If the top begins to brown too quickly during baking, tent with aluminum foil.

Remove the pan to a wire rack to cool for about 15 minutes. Then cut into 6 pieces and serve warm.

Makes 6 servings.

GINGERBEANBREAD
$1/2$ cup dried *azuki* beans

$3/4$ cup all-purpose flour, preferably unbleached

$1/2$ cup amaranth flour

$1/2$ teaspoon baking powder

$1/2$ teaspoon baking soda

$1/2$ teaspoon salt

$1/2$ cup unsulphured light molasses

$1/2$ cup sugar

$1/4$ cup ($1/2$ stick) unsalted butter, melted and cooled, or $1/4$ cup canola oil or other high-quality vegetable oil

1 egg

2 tablespoons finely chopped fresh ginger

GINGER CRUNCH TOPPING
2 tablespoons finely chopped fresh ginger

$1/2$ cup sugar

Fudgy Peanut-Oat Treats

½ cup unsalted butter

½ cup milk

2 cups sugar

¼ cup unsweetened cocoa powder,
   preferably Dutch-process type

½ teaspoon salt

¼ cup smooth peanut butter, preferably
   unsalted

1 teaspoon pure vanilla extract

1 cup unsalted, dry-roasted peanuts

2 cups rolled oats

Andrew recalls these old-fashioned confections as "witches' brew," a name he coined as a child while watching his mother stir up a caldron of the quick treats. Some old recipes identify this sweet combination of legume and grain as "no-bake cookies" or "boiled cookies." No matter what their name, these sweets set up very quickly. Be sure to measure and place all ingredients, along with waxed paper, alongside the stove top before beginning the recipe.

For variety, use any rolled grain or Sunshine Granola (page 35) in place of the oats.

In a large saucepan, combine the butter, milk, sugar, cocoa, and salt and place over high heat. Bring to a full boil, stirring constantly, and cook for 1½ minutes. Remove from the heat, immediately add the peanut butter and vanilla, and stir until smooth. Then quickly add the peanuts and oats and mix well. Working quickly while the mixture is warm, drop by tablespoonfuls onto waxed paper. Let cool until set.

Serve immediately, or cover tightly and store at room temperature for up to 2 days.

Makes about 3 dozen.

Spiced Bean Custard Pie with Buckwheat Crust

The pie in the photograph was made with Buckskin beans, an heirloom pinto grown by Native Americans in Montana, but almost any unseasoned cooked beans can be used. Black beans, however, may not be as visually appealing as brown, red, or white beans.

You may wish to double the crust and roll out half of it for cutting into geometric shapes, stars, leaves, or other fanciful designs. Position the decorations around the rim of the pie and brush with egg wash before baking. Or arrange the cutouts on a baking sheet and refrigerate until chilled, then brush with egg, bake at 350° F until crisp (about 15 minutes), and arrange over the top of the pie just before serving. For the photograph, the baked cutouts were lightly brushed with gold dust (available from stores that sell cake decorating supplies) mixed with a few drops of vodka.

To begin the Spiced Bean Custard Filling, if using dried beans, cook in water until very tender as directed on page 18 and set aside; do not season. If using canned beans, reserve for later use. Reserve the remaining filling ingredients for later use.

To begin the Vanilla Bean Cream, in a heavy saucepan, combine the cream and vanilla bean. Place over medium-low heat and warm the cream just until bubbles form along the edges of the pan; do not let it boil. Remove from the heat and let steep for about 20 minutes. Remove the vanilla bean and scrap the seeds into the cream. Transfer the cream to a metal bowl, cover, and refrigerate until well chilled. Reserve the sugar for later use.

To make the Buckwheat Crust, in a bowl or food processor, combine the flours, sugar, salt, and cinnamon and mix well. Add the butter and shortening and, using a pastry blender, fingertips, or a series of quick pulses with the steel blade of the food processor, cut as quickly as possible into the flour mixture until it resembles coarse bread crumbs. If using a food processor, transfer the mixture to a bowl. Sprinkle 1/4 cup iced water over the mixture and, using a fork, blend just until the dough holds together when pinched with your fingertips. The dough should be crumbly but not dry. If the mixture seems too crumbly, add more iced water, 1 tablespoon at a time.

→

SPICED BEAN CUSTARD FILLING

3/4 cup dried beans, or 1 1/2 cups canned beans (see recipe introduction)

About 1 1/4 cups heavy (whipping) cream, light cream, or canned evaporated milk

3 eggs

1 egg yolk

1 cup packed brown sugar, palm sugar, or maple sugar

2 teaspoons ground cinnamon

1/2 teaspoon ground allspice

1/2 teaspoon freshly grated nutmeg

1 teaspoon salt

2 teaspoons pure vanilla extract

VANILLA BEAN CREAM

1 cup heavy (whipping) cream, preferably not ultrapasteurized

1 vanilla bean, split lengthwise

About 2 tablespoons granulated sugar, preferably superfine, or powdered sugar

BUCKWHEAT CRUST

1 cup all-purpose flour, preferably unbleached

1/2 cup buckwheat flour

2 teaspoons brown sugar

1/2 teaspoon salt

1/2 teaspoon ground cinnamon

6 tablespoons very cold unsalted butter

3 tablespoons very cold solid vegetable shortening

1/4 cup iced water, or as needed

1 egg, lightly beaten, for brushing

Gather the dough into a ball, place on a sheet of plastic wrap, and press into a thick, flat disk about 5 inches in diameter. Bring the plastic wrap around to enclose the disk and refrigerate for about 15 minutes to "relax" the dough for a more tender crust.

Remove the chilled pastry from the refrigerator, unwrap, and place it in the middle of a piece of waxed paper about 12 inches square. Cover the pastry with a second sheet of waxed paper and allow to soften for about 5 minutes. Using a 9-inch pie pan as a guide, roll the dough from the center toward the edges, reducing the pressure as you near the edges, to form a round about 2 inches larger than the top of the pan and about 1/8 inch thick. Pick up and reposition the waxed paper between rolls to prevent sticking and replace it if it becomes too wrinkled. (Instead of using waxed paper, the pastry can be rolled out on a lightly floured, smooth work surface with a flour-dusted rolling pin.) If the dough breaks during rolling, brush the tear with a bit of cold water and cover with a piece of rolled dough cut from the edge of the circle. Avoid rerolling, as it toughens dough.

Discard the top sheet of waxed paper. Invert the dough into a 9-inch pie pan and peel away the waxed paper. Beginning at the center of the pan and working toward the edges and up the sides, press the dough lightly into the pan with your fingertips. Using a small sharp knife or kitchen scissors, cut the edge of the pastry so it hangs evenly about 1 inch beyond the outer edges of the pan. Fold the dough down over itself toward the inside of the pan. Smooth the perimeter with your fingertips to form a thick raised rim. Shape attractive edges by pinching the dough to create flutes, points, scallops, or other designs. Cover with plastic wrap and refrigerate until well chilled.

Preheat an oven to 400° F.

Cut a sheet of baking parchment or aluminum foil about 2 inches larger than the diameter of the pie. Press it into the pastry shell and fill it with pie weights, dried beans, or rice. Bake until the rim of the crust feels just set to the touch, 7 to 10 minutes. Remove from the oven and carefully lift the parchment or foil and the weights from the crust.

Using a fork, prick the bottom and sides of the pie crust in several places. Return the shell to the oven. Bake until the crust is almost done but not browned, 5 to 10 minutes longer; check the crust several times during baking and prick again with a fork if it puffs up. Brush the inside of the pie shell with some of the beaten egg and place in the oven for about 2 minutes to dry the egg. Transfer to a work surface.

Reduce the oven to 350° F.

To complete the Spiced Bean Custard Filling, drain the beans and transfer 1½ cups to a food processor or blender. (Cover and refrigerate or freeze any remaining beans for another purpose.) Purée the beans as smoothly as possible, adding up to ¼ cup of the cream or milk to facilitate puréeing. (For a smoother custard, grind or press thick-skinned beans through a food mill, sieve, or conical *chinois* after puréeing to remove the skins.) In a mixing bowl, lightly beat the eggs and egg yolk, then add the bean purée, 1 cup cream or milk, sugar, cinnamon, allspice, nutmeg, salt, and vanilla and mix well.

Pour the filling into the warm pie shell. Loosely cover the rim of the pastry with aluminum foil strips to prevent overbrowning. Bake until a knife inserted into the center comes out clean, about 45 minutes. Transfer to a wire rack to cool.

Shortly before serving, complete the Vanilla Bean Cream. Using a wire whisk or hand-held electric mixer, beat the chilled cream just until it begins to thicken. Add the sugar and continue to beat the cream until it holds its shape. Be very careful not to overbeat when using a mixer.

Serve the pie warm or at room temperature with the Vanilla Bean Cream.

Makes one 9-inch pie; serves 6 to 8.

RECIPE INDEX

INDEX TO RECIPES FEATURING BEAN & GRAIN COMBINATIONS IN OTHER JAMES McNAIR COOKBOOKS

ACKNOWLEDGMENTS

All dishes, glassware, flatware, and linens have been graciously provided by Vanderbilt and Company, St. Helena, California.

To the entire staff of Chronicle Books for their continued good work on my behalf.

To Sharon Silva, copy editor, for her critical eye and editorial proficiency.

To the panel of recipe tasters who sampled and evaluated dishes as Andrew and I prepared them along the way: Carol and Tom Bernot; Gretchen Eichinger and Michele Sordi; Karla Filler; Maile and Mark Forbert; Naila, Bill, and Harold Gallagher; Hank Julian and John Nyquist; Marian May and Louis Hicks; Martha and Devereux McNair and John and Ryan Richardson; and Sandra, Jim, Daniel, and Timothy Moore.

To Charles Gautreaux and John Nyquist and their friendly staff at Vanderbilt and Company for the generous loan from their collection of colorful European pottery and other tableware.

To Cleve Gallat of CTA Graphics for converting my design ideas into pages.

To Lucille and J. O. McNair, my parents, for all the beans, grains, and good times shared around the table over the years.

To Beauregard Ezekiel Valentine, Joshua J. Chew, Michael T. Wigglebutt, Miss Vivien "Bunny" Fleigh, and Miss Olivia de Pusspuss for their constant encouragement.

To Andrew Moore, my partner, for sharing equally with me the responsibility of developing, testing, and writing these recipes, and for his enthusiastic support that keeps me going. His skills and devotion are unsurpassable.